A Quiet Center

A Quiet Center

A Woman's Guide to
Resting in God's Presence

Susan Scott Sutton

kregel
PUBLICATIONS

Grand Rapids, MI 49501

A Quiet Center: A Woman's Guide to Resting in God's Presence

© 1999 by Susan Scott Sutton

Published by Kregel Publications, a division of Kregel, Inc., P.O. Box 2607, Grand Rapids, MI 49501.

Unless otherwise indicated, Scripture taken from the *Holy Bible: New International Version*®. Copyright © 1973, 1978, 1984 by International Bible Society. Used by permission of Zondervan Publishing House. All rights reserved.

Scripture quotations marked NASB are from the *New American Standard Bible*, © the Lockman Foundation 1960, 1962, 1963, 1968, 1971, 1972, 1973, 1975, 1977.

Library of Congress Cataloging-in-Publication Data
Sutton, Susan Scott.
    A quiet center: a woman's guide to resting in God's presence / by Susan Scott Sutton.
        p.   cm.
    Includes bibliographical references.
    1. Christian women—Religious life.   I. Title.
BV4527.S87   1999   248.8'43—dc 21   99-34888
                                                                    CIP

ISBN 0-8254-3662-1

Printed in the United States of America

3 4 5 6 7 / 09 08 07 06 05

To Betsy and Marnie
for the years we were together,
seeking to be all He calls us to be

Contents

Acknowledgments

A. W. Tozer wrote, "The only book that should ever be written is one that flows up from the heart, forced out by the inward pressure." And so this book began during a furlough year in the States. But that was just the beginning. In order to get further than the "inward pressure," it needed the patient and wise help of others, both in the States and in Chad, where it was finished. My heartfelt thanks to:

Jim Mignard, the first to nudge me toward writing the things that were on my heart. You made me believe I could do it.

Sheila Norris, Leslie Venable, and Lisa Grammon, who patiently read those first efforts when there must have been more pressure than art! Thanks for giving your honest critiques and encouragement.

Wendy Castle, who came all the way from England to Chad to visit a daughter and ended up giving precious hours to typing revisions of the manuscript. Since those revisions were made in pencil while riding along the bumpy dirt roads of Chad, you did wonders to make sense of the mess. Thanks for your willingness to serve.

The staff at Kregel, especially Dennis Hillman, who worked patiently with an author on the other side of the ocean and gave me the encouragement I needed along the way.

And last, because it means the most, my deepest thanks to Louis, who always gave me just the right word at just the right time. I am forever glad to be with you on the journey. "Glorify the LORD with me; let us exalt his name together" (Ps. 34:3).

Introduction

$\mathcal{T}$he spacious conference room hummed with eager voices as groups lounged by coffee tables and as individuals, just coming through the metal doors, greeted each other. All bore young, earnest faces as they waited expectantly for the speaker's arrival. Outside the conference hall, rambling paths extended silent invitations for quiet walks and reflective moments. A large lake sparkled in the early morning sun, flashing jewels brightly enough to turn heads. But on this morning no one turned to look wistfully through the open windows. Each made his or her way to a chair and turned toward the front of the room. Pens poised, bodies leaning forward, Styrofoam® cups, now half-drained of coffee, all were ready to hear and record the words of wisdom that would surely come.

A tall, white-haired woman stood before the group and placed her Bible on the podium. She was Barbara Boyd, a staff worker with InterVarsity Christian Fellowship (IVCF) and developer of the "Bible and Life" training weekends for students. The attentive faces in the room belonged to interns, staff-in-training with IVCF who were preparing for work on college campuses throughout the United States. I was one of those interns, eager to learn how to minister to students and to hear what the speaker had to say. Her subject was essential to the faith: the value of Scripture for our lives.

And so she began, "A long, long time ago my mother sat down inside."

Needless to say, these were rather strange words to begin a lecture. Heads raised in surprise, including my own. What did the speaker mean? As much as I respected her, I had not come to hear about her mother. Yet, as is often the case with lectures, I remember little else beyond those startling opening words. They will remain with me for the rest of my life, for they struck a chord in my heart. When I heard them, I knew God was inviting me to do the same, to sit down inside and live in my quiet center.

You can probably call to mind your own image of rest and security—a favorite soft armchair, an ocean-front cottage at dawn, a mountain ledge overlooking the green valley below. My stateside image is a bright bay-window seat, stuffed with comfortable cushions and strewn with inviting books. The view outside the window is of trees, hiding the busy world and cloistering me in as I sit and read with the sun's warmth on my arms.

Such images do help us to visualize a dwelling place of peace. They can only go so far, however, in suggesting what God has in mind when He invites us to rest. God is not speaking of a physical place where we temporarily escape the demands or dangers of the real world, but a spiritual place where we rest in the midst of the world. He invites us to Himself. He wants to become the quiet center of our lives where we can sit down and rest, that innermost "place" where we dwell secure, no matter what storms, confusion, or battles swirl around us.

This invitation came nearly twenty years ago, and my life has changed since then. Yet through the many changes—from single woman to wife to mother and, the most recent, to missionary—one thing has remained constant: No matter where I live or what I am doing, there is always the need to find my quiet center.

The Lord has taught me many lessons throughout my years with Him. Some of those lessons are ongoing, either because they are essential to the faith or because I'm a slow learner. The dearest ones have been forged in the fires of adversity, and it has often been during those heated times of difficulty that the Lord Himself has seemed most dear. It has also been in those times that He has taught me most fully how to rest.

During a recent furlough in the States, I shared some of these lessons on several occasions. I realized from my travels and speaking opportunities that there are many women who have a sincere desire to grow in faith but don't know how. They have never had the privilege of being in a fellowship or church that taught some of the basics of a personal relationship with God. So a desire grew in my heart to write down the lessons for those women who hunger for more in their faith and who might identify with my personal journey. This was followed by another desire to open up to the reader the great world of spiritual classics. I have a passion for quotes, especially from writers of the past. We have much to learn from those who have gone before. Not all of the quotes in this book are from the classics, and I only touch the surface with the ones quoted here, but all, I hope, will stimulate anyone who reads them to reach for the works of the spiritual mothers and fathers of the past.

I have also included at the end of each chapter some guidelines for spending time alone with God. No book is worth reading more than the Bible, and my words mean nothing unless they lead the reader to the Lord Himself. Mine is a simple book with basic truths, but I pray that it will lead the reader to the deep, satisfying, and life-changing truths of God's Word.

God knows our needs, and He can meet them. He calls us to seek and find who He *is*, who He *can be*, and who He *wants to be* for women in these busy days. He invites us to find our quiet centers.

> Nothing of man is sure, but everything of God is so. . . . He did not speak mere words. There is substance and truth in every one of His promises. . . . That which we have not yet received is as sure as that which has already come; therefore, let us wait before the Lord and be still.
> —Charles H. Spurgeon

1

God's Invitation

❧

We may rest assured that He who made us for Himself, that He might give Himself to us and in us, that He will never disappoint us. In waiting on Him we shall find rest and joy and strength and the supply of our every need.

—Andrew Murray

In you they trusted and were not disappointed.
—Psalm 22:5

Thomas Kelly, a Quaker missionary and scholar, wrote in his spiritual classic, *A Testament of Devotion*, "Deep within us all is an amazing inner sanctuary of the soul, a holy place, a Divine Center, a speaking Voice to which we may continuously return."[1] There is a place where we can go to rest. That resting place, or "Divine Center" as Kelly suggests, is not some higher level of spirituality nor a mystical feeling to attain. It is God Himself inviting us to continuously return to Him and rest.

The psalmist in the Old Testament understood this need to draw near to God and cried out to Him, "Be Thou to me a rock of habitation, to which I may continually come" (Ps. 71:3 NASB).

God answered that cry time and again throughout the centuries, but His final answer came through Jesus as an invitation:

> Come to me, all you who are weary and burdened, and I will give you rest. Take my yoke upon you, and learn from me, for I am gentle and humble in heart, and you will find rest for your souls.
> —Matthew 11:28–29

When we receive an invitation, we usually check the return address to see who sent it. Is it worthy of our consideration? Can we trust the one who has extended the invitation to fulfill any expectations we might have in responding? God's invitation holds a promise: "You shall find rest for your souls." Can we believe Him?

The question of trust is worth asking. Have you ever sat on a chair, only to have it dump you flat on the ground? I have, and I am not likely to relax again on a chair that looks or feels unstable! Neither will I be able to sleep peacefully in a tent during a thunderstorm. I've tried, but the flimsy canvas that surrounds me doesn't inspire trust that it will keep out the forces trying to get in. I rest fully only when I am able to trust what is holding me up or surrounding me.

Likewise, the foundation for resting in the Lord is trusting Him. How do I know that God is worthy of my trust, that when I respond to His invitation, I will, indeed, find rest for my soul? We can trust, because His invitation is backed by His character. When we consider His credentials, we find that He is worthy to fulfill His promise of rest.

Because He Created Us

God is the One who put us together, so He knows us extremely well and He knows best how we are to function. As Creator, He made us for a purpose, to belong to Him. "Know that the LORD is God. It is he who made us, and *we are his*" (Ps. 100:3, emphasis mine).

Have you noticed how often a baby is restless if held by someone other than his own mother? Likewise, our God-created life rests most fully in the arms of its Creator. St. Augustine wrote, "Thou hast made us for Thyself and our souls are restless until they find their rest in Thee." The psalmist, centuries before Augustine, acknowledged, "My soul finds rest in God alone" (Ps. 62:1).

Corrie ten Boom once spoke with a group of young people who were having difficulty maintaining a strong faith. "When I was a watchmaker," she counseled, "sometimes I had new watches that did not run well. I did not repair them myself, but returned them to the manufacturer. When he repaired them, they ran perfectly. This is what I do with my faith." She continued, "Jesus is the Author and Finisher of my faith. If it does not work well, I return it to the heavenly Manufacturer. And when He has repaired it, it works perfectly!"[2]

The Watchmaker of our souls knows best how to keep them running as they should. When we come to the One who created us and are in a relationship with Him, we can be fulfilled and at peace.

Because He Knows Us

"O LORD, you have searched me and you know me," David, Israel's shepherd-king, began in Psalm 139. He went on to contemplate the extent of God's knowing. "You know when I sit and when I rise; you perceive my thoughts from afar. You discern my going out and my lying down; *you are familiar with all my ways*" (emphasis mine).

David was comforted and encouraged by God's complete knowledge of him. We can take heart as well. God is intimately acquainted with all our ways, all our longings, all our weaknesses and strengths. Nothing that springs from our minds or emotions or lips can surprise Him. There is no temptation or failure that He has not seen or dealt with previously. Before God we have nothing to fear, nothing to prove, and nothing to hide.

J. I. Packer, in his modern-day classic *Knowing God*, writes of the tremendous impact this truth of God's all-knowing should have on our lives:

> This is momentous knowledge. There is unspeakable comfort—the sort of comfort that energizes, be it said, not enervates—in knowing that God is constantly taking knowledge of me in love, and watching over me for my good. There is tremendous relief in knowing that His

love to me is utterly realistic, based at every point on prior knowledge of the worst about me, so that no discovery now can disillusion Him about me, in the way I am so often disillusioned about myself, and quench His determination to bless me.[3]

Packer goes on to say that we should be humbled by the realization that God knows the worst about us. This full knowledge of our character keeps us honest about ourselves. It also sets us free. Since God knows all about us, we do not need to pretend before Him. We come to Him as we are and rest in His "utterly realistic" love.

Because He Loves Us

To be known so completely could be uncomfortable, except that the One who knows us this intimately also loves us perfectly. "I have loved you with an everlasting love," God declares, "I have drawn you with lovingkindness" (Jer. 31:3). God draws us to Himself not because we deserve it, but because He loves us with an everlasting love.

I remember when the truth of this verse dawned on my own restless heart. As a college student I was active in a campus fellowship, busy in leadership, and seeking to be all I thought God wanted me to be. There was a problem, though. As hard as I tried, the reality of who I was never fit with my ideals of who I should be. So I was never satisfied or at peace with myself and never fully sure of God's love. How could He love me when I was always falling short of His standards?

One day a friend drew my attention to the wording of Jeremiah 31:3 to explain the quality of God's love. God said to Israel, "I have loved you with an everlasting love," not "I will love you *if . . .*" He had set His love on His people before they ever had an opportunity to earn that love. God loved them by His choice, not by their merit. They never deserved it, neither before they entered into a relationship with God nor after. We know from reading the Old Testament that Israel's history is one of continual failure to live worthy of such a love, yet God's love for them, despite their waywardness and weakness, never ceased. He rebuked them, disciplined them, and allowed their sin to suffer its consequences, but He never stopped loving them or drawing them to Himself.

When I realized in those college days the quality of God's love, a new peace filled my heart and mind, and it changed my relationship with Him. Instead of being unsure of God because I related His love to my level of spiritual performance, I began to relax in His presence. I began to enjoy more fully my relationship with Him. I rested in the joy of being loved by God.

God has not changed throughout the centuries. This love, still undeserved and still unwavering, is available to us today. Knowing this wonderful truth, we can sing with assurance the beautiful line of a hymn by George Matheson, "O Love that will not let me go, I rest my weary soul in Thee." What freedom there is in coming to the One who knows us best yet loves us most, to a place where we are perfectly understood and perfectly loved. The cry of the heart today is to be understood and accepted. "Listen to me, love me, accept me!" God offers us the very things we long for most.

Because He Is Truth

The world offers an attractive smorgasbord of beliefs and lifestyles for the tasting. We are inundated in today's society with a "pick-and-choose" menu while being encouraged to agree that every item on display is a valid choice. Personal preference is what counts, not healthy choices. Such a menu may work in restaurants, but if this "all-you-can-eat" attitude is applied to life, that life becomes as unhealthy as a child who has learned only to indulge herself. Selfishness reigns, and self-control or limits of any form are labeled "old-fashioned," "intolerant," or "narrow-minded." Few people want to be told how to live today.

This presents a problem, of course. When every option in life is considered valid, truth becomes irrelevant. It is not merely lost in the crowded list of offerings, it is wiped off the menu. Or so it seems.

The essence of truth is that it remains truth whether or not it is acknowledged or accepted. Truth is not negotiable, or it has ceased to be truth. It can never really be wiped off the menu, though it can be ignored.

The *New Scribner-Bantam English Dictionary* defines truth as "conformity with fact; correctness, accuracy; something real and actual." Even better is the dictionary's definition of "reality." "Reality is what is, despite appearances." I like that. *Reality is what is.* It hints of God's answer to Moses when asked by the hesitant hero of Israel what His name was. "God said to Moses, 'I AM WHO I AM'" (Ex. 3:14). There is nothing to be added after such an answer. I do well to remind myself daily that, despite appearances, God is who He is.

Truth does not change with the times, and neither does God. Throughout history, He remains the eternal "I AM." "I the LORD do not change" (Mal. 3:6).

Truth is not relative. If it can change with circumstances, it is not truth but opinion, which is personal and subject to change. Neither do our circumstances change the character of God. Blaise Pascal, the seventeenth-century French theologian, philosopher, and mathematician, acknowledged even as he suffered a long and difficult period of ill health that "the altering of my condition can in no way alter Thine. Thou art ever the same, though I am subject to change."

In scientific terms, God is the constant and the world is the variable. We observe the latter all the time. Changing fashions, changing educational theories, changing parenting methods, changing health trends; one does not need to live long to see established re- search refuted and replaced by another set of "facts." Humans are indeed fickle creatures, willing to be tossed about in an ocean of trends rather than be an- chored on truth. In the midst of life's sophisticated confusion, no wonder we hear the disillusioned cry, "Whom can we believe?"

There is an answer to that cry. There is a source of truth that has never changed and never will: the Word of God.

Long ago I learned from your statutes that you
established them to last forever. . . . All your words
are true; all your righteous laws are eternal.
—Psalm 119:152, 160

> *I have not spoken in secret, from somewhere in a*
> *land of darkness; I have not said to Jacob's*
> *descendants, "Seek me in vain." I, the* LORD,
> *speak the truth; I declare what is right.*
> —Isaiah 45:19

Despite attempts throughout history to dilute, discard, or discredit it, God's truth about Himself, about ourselves, and about the world in which we live is eternal and constant. It is one truth we can always count on.

Because He Is Able

Our Chadian friends know this well, and they live by it. They depend heavily on God's mercies as they plant their fields and look to the heavens for the necessary rain. Because there is so much in their lives that they cannot control, living as close to nature as they do, they have no problem acknowledging a higher control. One of the most commonly used phrases in their vocabulary, for both the Christian who speaks Arabic and the Muslim, is "Allah ga'id." *God is.* There it is again, that universal truth which transcends place and culture. The Chadians use this expression for many occasions, but the most common is to affirm that, no matter what the circumstances, God is able. For the Muslim, this expression is more a resignation to fate than a hope, because Muslims view God as capricious and distant. Not knowing the God of the Bible, they do not believe He is personally involved in their lives. For our Christian friends, who know God intimately, it is an affirmation of faith. They have received His help often enough to know that He is able.

We in the Western world are in danger of losing this certain affirmation of faith. Because we are able to do so much for ourselves, God's enabling falls by the wayside. When society is advanced enough to penetrate the mysteries of space, divine assistance seems old-fashioned and unnecessary. Rather than giving recognition to the One in whom "all things hold together" (Col. 1:17), our modern society races forward with the smug assurance that a better life is somewhere around the corner, able to be attained through improved technology and enlightened minds. However, these amazing technological advances only gloss the surface of life. They fail to touch the underlying condition of the world. One only needs to study history and read each morning's newspaper to realize this is so. Time relentlessly marches past the grandstand of latest technology, while in the crowd beyond the stadium, war wages, famine occurs, poverty remains even in the wealthiest of nations, and people are still seeking peace within.

While this attitude of self-sufficiency in the stadium scoffs openly at the very notion that mankind needs God, it creeps subtly into the Christian arena as well. When the material world is comfortable and sufficient to meet our needs and when we can, indeed, provide so much for ourselves, even we as believers push God's sufficiency into a corner of our minds.

Saddened by the recent troubles of a close friend, I wanted to help her in some way, but living in a different town made any practical efforts difficult. I felt anxious for her and frustrated as I cast aside ideas, one by one, knowing none of them was feasible. What could I

do for her? A quiet voice, more like a thought, pen-
etrated my feeling of helplessness. *You can pray for her.*
What? I was about to brush it aside, because I had already prayed. The thought persisted. *Pray for her.* Of
course I will, but, Lord, I want to *do* something! *I beg
your pardon?* Well, You know, Lord, something that really helps. *As I said* . . . Sheepishly I realized what God
was bringing to my attention. Prayer is the most practical action we can take to help. Somehow I had forgotten, in my desire to be useful, that even though I
couldn't be present to help my friend, God could. So I
made my list, this time of ways to pray for her. I prayed
for her regularly and specifically, imagining God's
presence with her. In trusting her to God's care, peace
soon replaced frustration, and I rested from my anxiety. Later, I was able to rejoice with her as she acknowledged God's faithfulness in her situation.

Finding solutions to a problem does require action
on our part, but in seeking to be practical, we often
forget that prayer is one of the most practical options
we have. How is praying for someone practical? Because prayer brings into a situation the God of the
universe, all-knowing, all-wise, and all-powerful. Praying in earnest, however, is often the last option we
pursue. We either pray automatically without much
thought, or we relegate prayer to the Sunday service
or weekly Bible study. Prayer in this way becomes pas-
sive, little more than a Christian activity, rather than
active, bringing the living God into a situation. Thus,
having formed the habit of doing for ourselves (and
leaving God to our Christian gatherings), when something happens that becomes more than we can handle,

whether it be a major crisis or simply an unexpected event during the day, we have lost sight of God's sufficiency in the here and now. So when we finally do pray, we pray without truly believing and come away from prayer without peace.

When we doubt God will work in a situation—any situation—we are doubting either His goodness (that He will do something) or His power (that He can do something). We have allowed our minds to whittle God down until He becomes too small to meet our needs. If we cannot trust God's ability to help in any situation, perhaps we have lost sight of who He is and we need to reintroduce ourselves. We need to know Him better.

An Invitation

God invites us to do just that, to come to Him and get to know Him. When we respond to His invitation, we experience for ourselves His adequacy and we discover for ourselves that He is true to His Word. God has no need to prove Himself to anyone, but as we come to know Him intimately through His Word and in a personal relationship, He graciously proves Himself over and over again. We begin to trust Him more fully, and we are better able to be at rest.

J. I. Packer states, "There is no peace like the peace of those whose minds are possessed with full assurance that they have known God, and God has known them, and that this relationship guarantees God's favor to them in life, through death, and on forever."[4]

What wonderful and freeing truths! The God of the universe who created us to belong to Him, all-knowing, all-loving, all-able invites us to come to Him and to know Him.

This invitation is not a casual one. It is not meant for perusal with the rest of the mail stacked on our desk. Because each invitation is personal, an R.S.V.P. is attached. Just as responding to an invitation is necessary to benefit from what is offered, we must respond to God to receive His benefits. It is not enough to agree that this is good, to appreciate the opportunity and determine to get to it when we can. Neither is it enough to give a quick call of thanks for the thought. "Jesus on the telephone" can be a fun chorus for children's Sunday school, but it does not reflect the relationship that God desires. His invitation is personal, for this day of our lives, no matter how busy we are or how far from Him we feel. He waits for us to respond and to find our rest, our strength, our joy, and our quiet place in Him.

∽

Miriam watched from her window as a new neighbor moved in across the street. She liked the look of the young woman who, carrying potted plants, entered the vacant house. Wearing jeans and an oversized sweatshirt with the sleeves pushed up to her elbows like someone who meant business, the woman moved steadily in and out through the front door. She looked competent and friendly. Miriam noticed her laughing with the workers from the moving company while directing them where to take the boxes. A little while later, she glanced out the window again and saw the woman open a cooler and produce a variety of canned soft drinks. She then watched her lean over a picnic basket beside the cooler and pull out what looked like a plateful of brownies when the aluminum foil had been unwrapped. Miriam noted the pleased expressions on the faces of the workers as they each received the unexpected refreshments.

"I'd like to get to know her," Miriam thought before she turned away from the window to finish her Saturday to-do list.

During the next week Miriam glanced at the house across the street each morning as she drove out of her driveway to go to work. Once in the late afternoon as she was pulling groceries out of her car trunk, she saw the new neighbor working in the front yard. The woman looked up and gave a friendly wave; Miriam waved back with a smile as she headed for her front door.

"I do want to get to know her," she said to herself, "but now is not the time. I'm bushed and these groceries need to be put away. On Saturday I'll go over for a chat."

But on Saturday the new neighbor was away for the weekend. Miriam herself had planned to plant flowers in her back yard and didn't mind the delay; she had so much to do. She did, however, manage to chat across the bushes with Mrs. Pullam, her next door neighbor who had already met the new woman. Miriam listened with interest to what Mrs. Pullam had to say and she learned quite a bit, since Mrs. Pullam prided herself on knowing as much as she could about the neighborhood. Miriam learned that the new neighbor's name was Lauren Meersen and that she and her husband had moved from Florida. He was actually Belgian by birth and his company had recently built a huge complex on the edge of town. Lauren was American and who knows how they met, but what was most interesting was that Lauren was a poet. (Miriam brightened on this point because she herself was interested in poetry.) In fact, and the neighbor's eyes gleamed with importance as she relayed the next information, Lauren apparently had already published several books of poetry and was considered quite successful as a writer. In our own neighborhood! She was, by the way, going to teach at the local college when classes began in the fall.

Miriam left Mrs. Pullam tending her roses and decided she liked this new neighbor even more. And now she knew her name. She could think of her now as Lauren and not just the "new neighbor."

That afternoon Miriam went to the local bookstore to see if they had any books of poetry written by Lauren Meersen. They didn't, but they were glad to order one for her. Miriam told them about Lauren teaching at the college and suggested they order several copies. They agreed heartily, and she returned home, feeling satisfied for having been able to tell such interesting news and, at the same time, promote Lauren's writing. She was beginning to feel as if she already knew her neighbor. During the following week she waved every time she saw Lauren across the street.

The bookstore called the next Saturday to say that the book, *Once a Garden*, had arrived. Miriam had intended to run across the street and ring Lauren's doorbell, but when she finally got up from her computer, she was too eager to buy the book, so she headed to the store. She was quite pleased to see they had several copies on display.

When she returned home, she sat down in her favorite armchair by the picture window in her front living room. With a cup of hot raspberry-lemon tea in hand, she opened the book and began to read, eagerly at first, but then slowly, for they were the kind of poems that invited a walk, not a run. And as she read the poems, savoring them with the tea, Miriam felt that she was, indeed, walking in a garden. An hour passed before she knew it, because the quiet of the garden had surrounded her heart. When the last of the tea remained cold in her cup, she looked up from the words before her and felt she now truly knew her neighbor.

"I must go over tomorrow afternoon and tell her how much I love her poems," she murmured.

But the next afternoon, Miriam remembered that she had wanted to go to the Spring Festival and it was such a beautiful day she thought it better to be outside than in, so she drove off in her car with a guilty glance at Lauren's house.

Another week went by as Miriam hurried to and from the office, waved at her new neighbor, each time with a little more sense of guilt for not having yet stopped by, and re-read some of the poems when she had time. She told her coworkers, and even her sister, Jennifer, who called from Washington, about Lauren, all based on her acquired knowledge. She even recommended Jennifer read the poems for herself. They were so uplifting.

A week later Jennifer called Miriam. "I went to the library and found a copy of the book. You're right. The poems are beautiful."

"Aren't they? They do something to my spirit as I read them," Miriam said. "I knew you'd like them."

"It must be great to actually live across the street from her," Jennifer said wistfully. "What's she like as a person? How often do you get to talk with her?"

"Well . . ." Miriam hesitated and glanced toward the window. She wished Jennifer hadn't asked.

"You have met her, haven't you?"

"Well, actually, I've not had a chance."

"You mean she lives right across the street, and you haven't even met her?"

"Well, no, I haven't had the chance. But I plan to," Miriam finished brightly.

Jennifer was silent for a moment, then said, "Well, you seem to know so much about her." Another pause. "I would think to know her would be so much better. And she's so close, so available."

After Miriam hung up the phone, she thought about her sister's words. Although Jennifer was making a simple observation, Miriam realized a deeper truth in them. There is a great deal of difference between knowing about someone and knowing them personally. All of this knowledge about her neighbor and all of this talking about her could not substitute for a relationship with her.

She picked up the book of poetry that now sat permanently on her coffee table and took it with her as she crossed the street. She only knocked once and the door was opened. Lauren greeted her with a surprised and pleased expression and immediately invited her in. Miriam glanced around as she was led through the house to a sunny back porch. She sighed with contentment as she sank into the soft cushion of a wicker chair surrounded by several large clay pots of geraniums. The muted blue, green, and yellow hues of the room joined with the sun coming in through glass walls to make her feel warm and welcome. Lauren brought in a tray of tea, and they talked together, getting to know each other. Lauren seemed to have all the time in the world for her, Miriam thought. She soon felt comfortable enough with Lauren to ask questions about certain poems and was delighted with Lauren's answers. Sometimes they were self-effacing, sometimes humorous, and sometimes they were so deep that Miriam felt she was floating slowly in a stream of clear, pure water that never threatened to drown, only pulled her along to some higher point. She was sorry when she had to leave, but Lauren insisted she come again and gave her a hug as she left. Miriam re-entered her own house with a lightness of spirit she hadn't felt in a long time.

In the weeks that followed, Miriam visited Lauren several times. Lauren, in turn, dropped by or called to chat. Once they went together to a poetry reading at the local book store. Miriam introduced Lauren to the locals gathered there as her friend, and at the ease with which she said the word "friend," she paused and looked shyly at Lauren. Lauren's brown eyes twinkled. She leaned over and whispered to Miriam, "Yes, I'm so glad I've come to know you. We are indeed friends."

That night, Miriam reflected on what makes a friend. She called Jennifer the next day and thanked her for the words of wisdom, unintended but well-spoken. "I realized that I knew a lot about her and could even talk about her to others, but I didn't know her. That comes from spending time together. And it is far better. Do you know, Jennifer, that we are now indeed friends?"

"Great, Miriam," Jennifer replied with a laugh. "So when can you introduce me? I'd like to know her, too."

Be Still Before God

How often do we as Christians know about God and even talk about Him with others, but do not know Him?

Spending time with God develops our relationship with Him. This devotional time has been called the morning watch, the quiet hour, or quiet time. It is a period of time set aside to meet alone with God. The point of quiet time is not to "get our daily Bible reading done" or to "do our praying," but to know God. We speak with God through prayer and He speaks to us through His Word. By reading His Word, we learn more of who He is, who we are, and how we are to live for Him daily. We learn what is on His heart so we can live by His priorities. He speaks to the individual circumstances of our lives, giving guidance, comfort, encouragement, and rebuke as a loving father does with a beloved child.

> Prayer is the expression of the human heart in conversation with God. The more natural the prayer, the more real He becomes. It has all been simplified for me to this extent: prayer is a dialogue between two persons who love each other.[5]
> —Rosalind Rinker

Focus your heart and mind on God and ask Him to speak to you.

Suggestion: Begin a spiritual journal. One idea is to write in your own words the essential message of each verse below. Record in the journal what God is teaching you at this time. You may simply want to state what is on your heart in the form of a written prayer.

- Micah 6:8
- Ephesians 1:17–19
- Jeremiah 9:23–24
- Philippians 3:7–10

Read these verses carefully and consider why God is worthy of our trust and of our commitment to His ways and purposes.

- Psalm 18:30
- Psalm 139:1–12
- Psalm 25:10
- Psalm 145:13–17
- Psalm 33:11
- Isaiah 40:25–31

～

Thou, Lord, alone art all Thy children need,
And there is none beside;
From Thee the streams of blessedness proceed;
In Thee the blest abide,
Fountain of life, and all abounding grace,
Our source, our center,
And our dwelling place.
                —Madame Jeanne Marie Guyon (1648–1717)

2

Where Do We Begin?

∽

For my part, I keep myself retired with Him in
the center of my soul as much as I can.

—Brother Lawrence

*The eternal God is a dwelling place, and
underneath are the everlasting arms.*

—Deuteronomy 33:27 (NASB)

he early hours of a sub-Saharan morning are
gentle and quiet. Even the roosters crow and donkeys
bray from a muffled distance. A cool breeze filters
through screened windows, and the sun debuts in
subtle tones. I sit in the corner of our darkened bedroom reading by a solar lamp propped in the window.
In the circle of its light, surrounded by the emerging
dawn, I meet with the Lord. "He awakens me morning by morning, wakens my ear to listen like one being taught" (Isa. 50:4).

This time alone with God is essential to my faith,

but it is never as long as I would like, especially if I happen to be slow to wake up. The new day soon clamors for attention. A donkey-transported load of sloshing water arrives and an early visitor calls at the door. I rush to put breakfast on the table, my husband hurries off to the hospital, and our three lively children begin their homeschooling lessons. The quiet moments by the window are pushed aside by the pressing details of another day.

Sigh. "At least the devotions provided a start for the day ahead," I tell myself and turn to the task at hand.

Unfortunately, the end of my devotions often becomes, despite good intentions, not a springboard to the day but an end to intimacy with God. Like the example of the man in James 1:23–24 who looks at his face in a mirror and immediately forgets what he's seen, I rise from my devotions, become caught up in the day's events, and later can hardly recall what I read or prayed. I settle into a daily version of the Sunday Christian, giving a nod to God's existence that barely affects the substance of my life.

God, thankfully, isn't satisfied with a daily boost to head me in the right direction. He offers much more for my life. He offers a vital relationship that accompanies me along the way. I don't have to leave Him at the door of the church or standing beside the chair with my devotional material, because He comes with me into the day, into the kitchen, the office, the park, or the store.

"Easier said than done," any woman today might mutter as she looks at the pile of work on her desk or as the telephone rings for the third time while she tries to prepare a meal. Yet there is a quiet center of the soul from which the busy woman can meet with strength and peace the demands of her days. It is found in a sustained relationship with God.

Willa Cather, an American author in the early 1900s, wrote about the simplicity and harshness of pioneer life. In her early years of writing, she received advice from another writer, Sarah Orne Jewitt, who counseled, "Find your own quiet center and write from that to the world." The Christian woman can heed this advice, not from a literary point of view, but from a living point of view. Find your own quiet center and live from that center in the world.

Hannah Whitall Smith, a Quaker writer and speaker, understood the need for a quiet center of the soul and made this truth practical by comparing her spiritual life to an actual dwelling place. She wrote in *The God of All Comfort* that "the comfort or discomfort of our outward lives depends more largely upon the dwelling place of our bodies than upon almost any other material thing. Similarly," she wrote, "the comfort or discomfort of our inward life depends upon the dwelling place of our souls."

Following this image of a dwelling place for the soul, she continued:

> Our dwelling place is the place where we live, and not the place we merely visit. It is our home. All the interests of our earthly lives are bound up in our home; and we do all we can to make them attractive and comfortable. But our souls need a comfortable dwelling place even more

than our bodies; inward comfort, as we all know, is of far greater importance than outward; and where the soul is full of peace and joy, outward surroundings are of comparatively little account.[1]

The Scriptures verify the image of God as our dwelling place:

> *Lord, you have been our dwelling place*
> *throughout all generations.*
>   —Psalm 90:1

> *He who dwells in the shelter of the Most High*
> *will rest in the shadow of the Almighty.*
>   —Psalm 91:1

> *The eternal God is a dwelling place, and under-*
> *neath are the everlasting arms.*
>   —Deuteronomy 33:27 (NASB)

The Bible speaks of God as a dwelling place in the images of a fortress, a high tower, and a refuge (Pss. 18:2; 31:3; 91:2; 144:2). A fortress is designed for security. It is meant to be a place of refuge from the enemy, but a refuge does me no good unless I am inside, dwelling within those strong walls. If I am inside a fortress where the walls are thick and the windows are high, then I can feel sure that the enemy is not going to enter and disturb my peace. If I step out of that fortress, however, I am inviting the enemy to have a field day with myself as the target.

A good question, then, and one I have to ask myself

from time to time as a spiritual check, is "Where am I living?"

Where is my emotional dwelling place? Where do my heart and mind live throughout the day? Are they settled in God's Word, which is associated with His being our refuge (Ps. 119:114), or are they wandering around outside of His fortress, providing target practice for the enemy of our souls?

Even being close by the fortress, enjoying a swim in the moat with the fortress in sight, isn't enough. Without the anchor of God's Word, soon enough my life becomes little more than a series of reactions to what goes on around me. My thoughts and emotions become like a cork on the water bobbing up and down, buoying me up or pulling me down with the circumstances. When this happens, my thoughts about myself, about those around me, and even about God become shaped more by the ever-changing circumstances of life than by the fortress of never-changing biblical truth. So I ride uncomfortably balanced on an emotional and spiritual wave, wondering how I got on and longing desperately to get off.

Most damaging of all is letting this ride on the waves shape my thoughts about God. When things are going well, God is good; when things are going poorly, God is cruel. When life gives me what I want or expect, God's in His heaven; when nothing goes the way I had hoped, I wonder where God is or if He cares. God has answered my prayers, praise the Lord; He hasn't answered yet, prayer doesn't work. Up and down, I measure God's goodness, power, faithfulness, or love by the comfort or discomfort in my life.

This tendency robs me of the peace and joy that God intends for those who come to Him in faith. When I determine His character by my life circumstances, I am exchanging reality for shifting shadows and, as the apostle Paul wrote, "the truth of God for a lie" (Rom. 1:25).

God never intends for us to live in the moat, riding precariously on the waves of faith and openly vulnerable to the enemy. When He invites us to Himself as a quiet center, He tells us to enter a fortress where the floor below us doesn't move and the walls around us never crumble.

God is not a visiting center. Hannah Whitall Smith observes that many Christians with a sincere faith tend to treat God not as a dwelling place but more as a place to visit.

> A great many people "run into" God's fortress on Sunday, and come out of it again as soon as Monday morning dawns. Some even run into it when they kneel down to say their prayers at night, and come out of it five minutes afterward when they get into bed. Of course, this is the height of folly. One cannot imagine any sensible refugee running into a fortress one day, and the next day running out among the enemy again. We should think such a person had suddenly lost all his senses. But is it not even more foolish when it comes to the soul?[2]

The key to true security is remaining in the fortress. The key to resting in the Lord is remaining in Him as our spiritual dwelling place. Jesus had this in mind when He said to His disciples, "Remain in me, and I will remain in you. No branch can bear fruit by itself; it must remain in the vine. Neither can you bear fruit unless you remain in me" (John 15:4).

Knowing that we are to remain in the fortress, that is, to remain in Christ, is a wonderful truth, but how to do so often eludes us. Hannah Whitall Smith admits, "It is comparatively easy to take a step of faith, but it is a far more difficult thing to abide steadfastly in the place into which we have stepped."[3] How true! I used to envision "abiding" as walking around with a saintly smile on my face and a Bible in my hand, exuding peace and greeting each disruption in life with calm and wisdom. This vision of heavenly mindedness lasted only as long as the daydream, because the realities of life never let me practice such saintliness! Thankfully, I never had the chance to practice, since I probably would have only looked foolish and I doubt that God means for us to live our days as absentminded saints. Besides, this reality that is ever before me forces me to offer to God who I am and not who I think I should be.

But the question remains. How do we abide? Jesus has commanded us to remain in Him and we are willing, but how do we experience this spiritual truth of abiding? Again, the image of an actual dwelling place helps to make it practical.

What makes the difference between a dwelling and a place we visit? When we have a place of our own, whether it be a house, apartment, or bedroom, we care for it and make it ours. We decorate and furnish it. Because we live in it, we don't let it deteriorate. We spend the time necessary to keep it comfortable, clean, and functioning. A place we visit, on the other hand, may bring momentary delight, but we do not expend time and effort to keep it that way. We enjoy it and we leave, usually giving no more thought to the place, except perhaps to retain fond memories of our visit.

We make the Lord our spiritual home by maintaining our relationship with Him, much as we would maintain a physical home. A house will not take care of itself, and neither will a relationship. Both require effort and time.

This decision to be serious about my spiritual dwelling may require, before anything else, an honest examination of my attitude toward God. How much do I truly care about Him? Apart from external Christian activities, past or present (attending church, small group Bible study, choir practice, prayer meetings), I must ask myself, how important is the Lord Himself in my life? Is my relationship with Him a priority, important enough to put time and effort into maintaining it?

This question is dear to God's heart. When a lawyer asked Jesus, "Teacher, which is the greatest commandment in the Law?" (Matt. 22:36), the young man was seeking to know God's priority among His own laws. To keep the Sabbath? To tell the truth? To fast and pray on a regular basis? To help the poor? There was a multitude of Jewish laws even beyond the Ten Commandments that Jesus could have quoted to answer this question, all of which were good and right to follow. But His response revealed what is ultimately on God's heart for those who seek Him. Jesus replied, "Love the Lord your God with all your heart and with all your soul and with all your mind" (Matt. 22:37). He directed the lawyer beyond duty and activity to intimacy and relationship.

We can be very busy for God outwardly, all in very good and right ways, while neglecting our inner relationship with Him.

I am one of those unfortunate souls who has a hard time when the house is a mess. I say unfortunate because, as a messy home is unavoidable with children, it means I am constantly in danger of losing my sanity. If the adage, "A woman sets the tone for the home," is true, this does not bode well for those who live with me while I'm frustrated with messiness! No mother can be a perfectionist and remain sane, so I do manage to live with a certain amount of disorder. (This is absolutely necessary in our home on the mission field, where dust storms regularly deposit a film of grit on every surface in the house.) Even so, every once in a while, in an effort to remedy both the state of my home and my spirit, I set myself in high gear and zip around like a determined speed skater to bring some order into a room, any room, as long as I can get it straightened up. Not everyone is this way, but I do function better with order around me.

Disorder in the home especially reigns when we have been too busy as a family outside the home. When the children miss their Saturday cleaning day, or when I am too busy to straighten up on a regular schedule, the external disorder increases to mammoth proportions. For any woman burdened with like affliction, only by maintaining order on a regular basis can the home be a place of rest, enjoyment, and fulfillment. Likewise, if I am not taking time to regularly maintain my internal relationship with God, no matter how busy

I might be on the outside with good and acceptable spiritual activities, there is no quiet center, no place of rest for my mind and heart.

Like the young lawyer, we sometimes look for something we can do to become better Christians. God tells us, instead, what we are to be: women in relationship with Him, loving Him with our very beings; a basic, yet essential truth, but so easy to stray from. It is sometimes beneficial to spend time alone with God and bring questions like the following before Him:

- Do I love you, Lord, in the way You have asked me to (with all my heart, soul, and mind)?
- How do I treat You each day—as the Sovereign of my day, or as an afterthought?
- Am I neglecting my relationship with You for other activities?

The woman who finds a quiet center in the midst of her busy life loves her Lord and seeks Him for all her needs. She is as committed to her spiritual dwelling as to her physical dwelling place. She recognizes that this commitment will require time and effort to maintain.

Many Christians with a sincere faith and a genuine desire to serve God have never entered this permanent spiritual place of residence. They have never gone beyond the idea of God as a divine visiting center. They live, even as Christians, still hungering, still thirsting, still not fully satisfied, still carrying baggage because they have not set it down in a permanent place.

Jesus says, in effect, "Come to Me, unpack your baggage, and stay."

Be Still Before God

> For he that dwelleth in God dwelleth in a peace-
> able habitation and in a quiet resting place.[4]
> —Hannah Whitall Smith

Take time to be still before God. What will He say to you today through His Word?

Suggestion: Read a psalm of praise to focus your heart and mind on the Lord.

Read the following verses and reflect on the image of God as our dwelling place. Then ask yourself, "Where am I living today?"

- Psalm 18:1–2
- Psalm 61:3–4
- Psalm 31:3, 20
- Psalm 90:1–2
- Psalm 32:7
- Deuteronomy 33:12, 27

Ꮗ

> In my creature impatience I am often caused to wish that there were some way to bring modern Christians into a deeper spiritual life painlessly by short easy lessons, but such wishes are vain. No short cut exists. God has not bowed to our nervous haste nor embraced the methods of our machine age. It is well that we accept the hard truth now: the man who would know God must give time to Him. He must count no time wasted which is spent in the cultivation of His acquaintance.
> —A. W. Tozer (1897–1963)

3

Be Available

c✦ɔ

The very first thing that we need to do is set apart
a time and a place to be with God and him alone.
The concrete shape of the discipline of solitude
will be different for each person.[1]

—Henri Nouwen

My soul thirsts for God, for the living God.
When can I go and meet with God?

—Psalm 42:2

*I*t takes time to make God a priority. Time is a precious commodity that we all wish we had more of, or
at least we'd like less to do in the time available to us.
I can hardly brush my teeth without someone or something clamoring for my attention. The student who
stays up late studying for an exam can barely get going in time for the next day's class. A professional
woman must rise early to go to work. A mother with a
job outside the home must not only get herself going

but her children as well. The mother whose career is homemaking rises early, not to meet with the Lord as she would like, but because her preschoolers are already up and going. How do we make ourselves available to God in a day full of people, occupations, and demanding responsibilities?

If we want to develop intimacy with God, the starting point is a commitment to make time for Him. Every river that flows serenely through mountains and valleys has a starting point. Without that continually replenishing source, the river eventually will become dry.

This is what happens in sub-Sahara Africa during three-fourths of the year. Rain falls only two or three months during the year in Chad. When the rains come, they flood the land until the underground water table is saturated. For three months, the rivers flow. Cattle, camels, donkeys, and sheep drink to their hearts' content. Grass springs from the dry, sandy terrain, changing the landscape considerably. The people anticipate a harvest of grain to feed their families throughout the coming year. But when the rains cease, it does not take long for those once-flowing rivers to become completely dry. During the nine remaining months, villagers stand waist deep in holes dug in sandy riverbeds, searching underground for a small pool of water to satisfy their thirst. With the absence of a source, the rivers cease to flow, leaving only a barren land. What a picture of our spiritual lives!

Jesus said, "Whoever believes in me, as the Scripture has said, streams of living water will flow from within him" (John 7:38). In order to have a continual stream, we need a continual source.

Spending time with God is the source of our own rivers of living water. We cannot "sit down inside" until we take the time to sit down with God. Yet finding time for personal devotions often seems impossible. One woman, Jean, dismisses a devotional life as possible only for those blessed few who can visit a retreat center. "Nice idea," she thinks, "but not practical. Maybe some day when I have more time." Her friend, Mary, knows the value of time with God, but can't seem to develop a consistent practice of devotions. "I get to it when I can."

Jean has never tapped into the source and is missing out on the abundant life God offers through knowing Him intimately. Mary is in danger of drying up spiritually because of sporadic contact with the source.

For a season, even after the rains have stopped, Chad's landscape remains green. Tomatoes flourish along the saturated riverbeds. The ground continues to be productive for a time because of the water that remains underground and in the riverbeds. But this fruitfulness is deceptive. Soon the water level drops and the land reveals its thirst. Likewise, we can run for a fairly long time on spiritual nourishment we have received in the past, whether that past was years ago in a Christian fellowship or last Sunday's sermon. But we cannot survive on past experience. We will become spiritually parched if we are not continually being replenished by the Source of Life. Lack of joy, lack of love for the Lord or for others, lack of commitment to His purposes in the world, lack of contentment and peace all reflect a parched soul.

The danger of spiritual thirst is even more subtle for

the woman involved in ministry. Gaining fulfillment from Christian service, she may fail to recognize when her love for the Lord Himself is growing cold. Doing His work keeps her too busy to sit at His feet. Preparing Bible studies in order to teach others takes the place of listening to the Lord for herself. Activities *for* Christ subtly replace intimacy *with* Him, and she finds herself outwardly radiant while inwardly weary. She has lost touch with the source.

All three women, Jean, Mary, and the woman active in ministry, may hope that one day they will find time for the essentials. Yet time never accommodates itself to our schedules. If we wait until we have time, we will keep waiting. The conveniences of today only free us up, it seems, for more activity rather than for rest. It seems impossible, then, to pursue a devotional life in the midst of this obstacle of time. Not so impossible, says the One who not only desires us to spend time with Him but gives us an example to follow. We learn from Jesus that meeting alone with God is not so much a matter of time but of the will.

If anyone had no time in His day for extras, it was Jesus. Even so, He made a habit of going away to be alone with God. He not only talked about the importance of an intimate relationship with God, He lived it.

Look at a typical day in the life of Jesus, as recorded in the first chapter of the gospel of Mark.

His day begins early, with the sunrise. Jesus spends the morning at the synagogue, not sitting comfortably in the listening crowd, not relaxing with his back against the wall, but standing before the crowd teaching. Neither can He teach the gathered group of men before Him in peace. The quiet, reverent, almost sleepy atmosphere explodes suddenly with a scream. All heads turn in surprise toward a demon-possessed man in the crowd who is suddenly hurling accusations at Jesus. The eyes then turn to Jesus to see how He will handle the situation. He doesn't disappoint them. Jesus confronts the evil spirit quickly and authoritatively with a display of power that both amazes and confuses the group before Him. Some, no doubt, run out of the synagogue, eager to relate what has just happened. Knowing how quickly news travels by mouth in our rural society in Africa, I am not surprised that Mark writes, "News about him spread quickly over the whole region of Galilee" (Mark 1:28).

But this dramatic point is only halfway through Jesus' day. He leaves the synagogue and walks to the house of Simon and Andrew, perhaps looking forward to a quiet lunch with his friends. He arrives to find, however, that lunch is not ready and Simon's mother-in-law is ill with a fever. And He is expected to do something about it. The household tells Jesus about the sick woman as soon as He arrives at the door. No time to rest, no time to wind down from the excitement He has just left behind at the synagogue. Once more, all eyes look to Jesus to see what He will do. And what does He do? He goes immediately to the sick woman and heals her.

Two miracles in one day is more than this town can bear quietly, so word spreads even more of this Jesus' abilities to heal, bringing more people to Him for help. Sunset comes, winding down the day. Jesus is still at the house. And so, it seems, is everyone else. Mark writes that "the whole town gathered at the door." The townspeople had brought to Jesus anyone who was ill or demon-possessed, begging for His time, attention, and energy. And He gave it.

Mark does not tell how late Jesus stayed up ministering. Yet true to His style of ministry, we know He did not wave a hand over the crowd and proclaim them all healed. We know from scriptural accounts that Jesus saw each person, listened to each problem, and took the time to speak to or touch each individual. Mark records that it was "very early in the morning, while it was still dark" when Jesus was able to do anything else. And what did He do? "Jesus got up, left the house and went off to a solitary place, where he prayed" (Mark 1:35).

Even if Jesus had actually slept before getting up early to pray, He still chose to get up though He was exhausted. The previous day would have drained Him emotionally, spiritually, and physically. The day to come would surely bring more of the same. He could be excused for lack of sleep. Yet He arose before anyone else in the house, because He knew the importance of meeting with God. If He was to find time alone with His Father, He would have to beat the crowds, and that meant getting up before dawn.

He also sought a place where He could be alone. This was probably not easy in a small town. The house itself, filled with people, would have been too small for privacy. He had to seek solitude outside the house, perhaps even beyond the town limits.

Jesus wanted to be alone with God, but doing so did not come easily. He had to find a time and a place, even if it meant a walk through town.

This is not a unique event in Jesus' life. Seeking time

alone with the Father was a regular practice. Luke records that "Jesus often withdrew to lonely places and prayed" (Luke 5:16). When He had to make important decisions, He took even more time to pray. The night before He named the twelve men into whom He would pour His life and teachings, He "went out to a mountainside to pray, and spent the night praying to God" (Luke 6:12).

Jesus was a busy man, sought after and rarely left alone, but His habits reveal that finding the time to meet with God was a matter of the will. When He could find no time during the day, He met with God before the day began or in the hours of the night.

When I look at my own schedule and hold it up to the light of Jesus' busy days, I see a lifestyle that needs an honest evaluation. I manage to find time for those things I genuinely want to do. So I must ask myself a question of the will. Is my relationship with God important enough for me to make an effort, no matter how busy I am and no matter where I am, to meet with Him?

Be Still Before God

Take time to quiet your mind and focus on His presence with you.

> Our real problem, in failing to center down, is not a lack of time; it is, I fear, in too many of us, lack of joyful, enthusiastic delight in Him, lack of deep-drawing love directed toward Him at every moment of the day and night.[2]
>
> —Thomas Kelly

Suggestion: Keep a notepad and pen beside you. Whenever a distracting thought comes (a person you need to call, a "to-do" list item), write it down so you won't forget, then let the matter rest and turn your thoughts fully to the Lord.

If you have begun a spiritual journal, write in your own words what the following verses say about our love for God and about His love for us.

- Deuteronomy 4:29
- Psalm 42:1–2
- Deuteronomy 6:4–5
- Psalm 43:4
- Deuteronomy 10:12–13
- Psalm 84:10–12
- Matthew 22:34–38
- Zephaniah 3:17

∽

Change of place does not effect any drawing nearer unto God, but wherever thou mayest be, God will come to thee if the chambers of thy soul be found of such a sort that he can dwell in thee and walk in thee.

—Gregory of Nyssa

4

Be Flexible

❧

Precisely because our secular milieu offers us so
few spiritual disciplines we have to develop our
own.[1]

—Henri Nouwen

*I rise before dawn and cry for help; I have put
my hope in your word. My eyes stay open
through the watches of the night, that I may
meditate on your promises.*

—Psalm 119:147–48

𝓘 am glad that God delights in variety. We need
only glance at nature to see how much He enjoys
individuality in His creation. God's creativity extends,
of course, to the human race. God created each of us to
be unique, and He relates to us as the individuals we
are. As Creator, He knows fully our individual
personalities, external schedules, and internal body
clocks. Because God knows intimately our frame and

schedule, we can be flexible in finding a time and place for devotions that suit our needs and give Him our focused time.

We hear most often, and I believe it to be true, that the best time to meet with God is in the morning. The well-known Bible expositor of the seventeenth century, Matthew Henry, stated his preference for morning devotions: "The morning is the first part of the day, and it is fit that he that is the first should have the first, and be first served."[2] One reason for spending time with God at the beginning of the day is to give Him a place of priority, to acknowledge that "he . . . is the first."

Matthew Henry also noted, "In the morning we are most free from company and business, and ordinarily have the best opportunity for solitude and retirement."[3] Too often an attempt later in the day is pushed aside by responsibilities that can't seem to wait. Many times they truly can't wait, so we ask God to wait until the evening. But by nightfall, we may be too tired to give our full attention. So, according to Henry, "It is the wisdom of those that have much to do in the world, that have scarce a minute to themselves all day, to take time in the morning before business crowds in upon them."[4]

Morning is likely the best time to meet with God for the reasons mentioned. For many of us, if we do not meet with God in the morning, we may not meet with Him at all. Still, a morning quiet time is not always possible. Not all of us can say with Matthew Henry, "If ever we be good for anything; it is in the morning."[5] Our body clocks may not function early enough, and the morning may not be the most alert time we can offer God. Or a job may begin in the wee hours of the dawn, allowing free time only in the afternoon or evening. A newborn baby allows no schedule at all. Does not the One who sees all know these things?

My own practice of quiet time has had an interesting and varied journey. I became a Christian in high school through a group that emphasized the devotional life. Excited about growing in Christ, I was eager to begin regular devotions. Still, as an active teenager needing to rise early for school and study at night, finding time wasn't easy. This was especially true the year that I decided to earn money by driving a school bus. After a few bleary-eyed mornings, my good intentions gave way to more sleep. I shifted devotions to the evening. Locating a place at home was sometimes difficult because I did not have a room of my own. Therefore, many nights I would sit on the floor of the bathroom adjoining my room after others had gone to bed. There I could read the Bible and pray without disturbing my sister, and I could feel truly alone with God.

As a university student, I had more control of my time. Devotions fit easily into the schedule of classes, but as the schedule changed from semester to semester, so did my time to meet with God. The place varied as well. When a semester included a free hour between classes, I was able to slip into the quiet Episcopal chapel on the edge of campus for an extended period of solitude. Its stone walls ushered me into Christ's presence where I could hear His voice in the midst of the university's noise. A white scrap of paper tacked onto my desk in the dorm bore a reminder: "I go out into

the world not to show who I am, but Whose I am."
Meeting regularly with God held me to that principle
and to His priorities during those years on a secular
campus.

Louis and I met on campus in the InterVarsity Christian Fellowship (IVCF), a Christian organization that
taught the importance of a vital relationship with God.
When we married after graduation, we established the
priority of "quiet time" as a couple. Knowing that a
strong individual relationship with God was important for a strong marriage, each of us met alone with
God in a separate room of the house. Finding this time
was easier for me than for Louis in those years. Working with students as I did while on staff with IVCF, I
planned my own schedule. He was a medical student
with sleepless nights and early mornings. But he carried a small New Testament to the hospital every day
so he could catch moments as they came for reading.
The minutes that Louis biked from the hospital to our
cottage on the other end of campus provided an opportunity for private conversations with the Lord.
Later, during his medical residency in family practice,
when we had moved to another state and the distance
between home and hospital was greater, the car became his chapel.

After our children were born, I joined Louis in fac-
ing sleepless nights and early mornings. I, too, started
catching the moments as they came. This was difficult
enough with the birth of Scott, our active son, but those
moments became increasingly scarce with the arrival
two years later of twin daughters, Susan and Elizabeth. The combination of a toddler and infant twins

produced busy days indeed. Thankfully, Susan and Elizabeth enjoyed being on the same schedule, so at times I could read the Bible and pray during their naps if Scott chose to join them. There were many days, though, that the moment of solitude did not come until the middle of the night when I was awakened by a cry. While rocking a child to sleep, I picked up the Bible and met with the Lord. At other times, when I didn't have enough energy to turn a page, a hymn sung softly to the child in my arms served also as a prayer. God understood the weariness of a mother in the night and blessed those moments with His presence.

During the toddler and preschool years, we often longed and even prayed for the children to sleep more, thinking we could have some minutes free in the morning. This hope never materialized and we would at times, unfairly, be frustrated with our children for not changing their schedules to suit our desires! One day we realized, prompted by the Holy Spirit, that maybe we should change our habits rather than wait for the children to change theirs. If we truly wanted to meet with God, then we had to make it happen. We set our alarm clocks to wake up earlier.

None of this was easy nor did we ever greet a morning with a bounce out of bed. Neither one of us is naturally inclined to begin the day singing heartily "All Hail the Power of Jesus' Name." But setting the alarm earlier and getting up when it rang was a matter of the will. Was God important enough for us to make the effort, or would we put Him at the back of an increasingly crowded shelf, only to reach for Him when we had enough time?

Now that our children are older, they understand our focus on this time alone with God. They have observed us enough throughout the years to know this time is as important as an appointment with a person they could physically see and are not to interrupt unless there is a genuine need. Still, the noises of a waking household, pressing activities of the day, and the exuberance of three teenagers all provide ample distraction. We still have to set the alarm and get out of bed, however slowly, to meet with the Lord if we are to have quality devotions. We still have to choose to make the time to meet with Him before the day's activities steal it away.

The years ahead will bring different circumstances and different schedules. The life of faith is a journey, and the road we travel winds, twists, and turns as the Lord directs our individual paths. We may have to be flexible once in a while and adjust our schedules, but we will always have a need for nourishment along the way. Our traveling companion is Christ Himself. Our food and drink is His Word. Meeting alone with Him is the coffee shop along the way, providing the direction we need and the strength to keep going. We do well to stop at regular intervals for rest and renewal, whether we meet with Christ in the morning or at some other time of the day or night.

Be Still Before God

If you are not currently having a "quiet time," think through your day and decide when you can set aside time to meet with God.

Ask: What do I need to do to have a quiet time?

- set my alarm to wake up earlier?
- tell someone who will help me be accountable to this commitment?
- find a place that is quiet and free of distractions?

Continue in your spiritual journal with these verses:

- Psalm 5:3
- Isaiah 50:4
- Psalm 119:2, 10, 147–48
- Jeremiah 29:13

↜

You will tell me that I am always saying the same thing. It is true, for this is the best and easiest method I know; and as I use no other, I advise all the world to do it. We must know before we can love. In order to know God, we must often think of Him; and when we come to love Him, we shall also think of Him often, for our heart will be with our treasure.

—Brother Lawrence

5

Be Connected

c━━o

It is a great thing to enter the inner chamber and shut the door and meet the Father in secret. It is a greater thing to open the door again and go out in the enjoyment of His presence which nothing can disturb.[1]

—Andrew Murray

This is the best way to act: talk a great deal to the Lord.[2]

—Frank Laubach

$\mathcal{P}$auline, a fellow missionary in Chad, was walking along the dirt road between her home and the town airport. The day was hot and dry, the air filled with a fine film of dust that settled on the skin. She noticed, as she walked uncomfortably in the heat, a single flower sticking out of the dirt. Its lovely, delicate blossoms caught her eye. Any flower that was tough enough to bloom above the hard surface of a near-desert roadside deserved respect. In fact, she thought that if it survived by that road, it might survive just as easily in her own yard, which was in need of plants to offset the stark surroundings.

Pauline stooped and placed her fingers gently around the flower's stem. She hoped to pull it out by the roots and transplant in her courtyard. Eyeing its frail stem, she was sure this would be an easy maneuver. She was wrong. However firmly she pulled, the plant wouldn't budge. She tugged harder and still couldn't pull it from its hard-packed base. So she locked her knees and pulled as firmly as she could without breaking the stem. The flower remained undisturbed in its place. By this time, Pauline was hot and sweaty and decided she had no need to expand her garden! Her instinct told her that the roots went too deep for her to be able to pull the plant out of its natural home. It was connected.

The flower had a hidden strength. Its surface environment was harsh, dry, and barren. No one came along regularly to care for it, to water and tend it. It had to survive in a climate that daily buffeted its petals with dust storms, hot winds, and scorching sun. It had to resist a force that was determined to move it from its appointed spot! Yet there it remained, delicate in beauty, frail outwardly, but, as Pauline discovered, tough inwardly. It survived, not because its outward environment was favorable, but because its root system went down deep enough to remain constantly in touch with the underground source that sustained it.

We have probably all felt like the flower at one time

or another. I know I have. Circumstances buffet my spirit. Pressures bend me under their weight. Forces beyond my control threaten to disconnect me from the hidden source. Like the flower, I may have tapped into the source of life, but I still have to do my living on the surface. Yet also, like the flower, I can remain steadfast despite the circumstances that surround me. The key for the flower was its continual connection with its source. If it could speak, it might well recite the poem:

> Nothing that happens can hurt me,
> Whether I lose or win.
> Though life may be changed on the surface,
> I do my main living within.

I try to do my "main living within" and be at rest on the surface. The key for me, like the flower, is to remain constantly in touch with my own hidden source of strength, which is Christ. Practically, that means going beyond the quiet of personal devotions into the busyness of the day and bringing Christ with me. It is too easy to leave Him sitting by the Bible on the chair while I get on with my day.

The truth is, of course, that He is always with me. He has never left my side. David, Israel's shepherd-king, knew this truth. "Because he is at my right hand," David wrote, "I will not be shaken" (Ps. 16:8). God is as close as my right hand, watching, caring, guiding, protecting, whether or not I am aware of it. It is, after all, one of His names—Emmanuel, "God with us."

C. S. Lewis stated, "We may ignore, but we can never evade, the presence of God. . . . The real labor is to remember, to attend." None of us, I imagine, means to deliberately ignore God's presence. We simply find it hard, in the rush of a day, to consciously remember that He is with us.

Christians throughout the centuries have received inspiration from the example of Brother Lawrence, a Carmelite monk who lived in the late 1600s in a continual awareness of the presence of God.[3] Brother Lawrence learned to practice the presence of God, not, as one might think, in the prayer chapel, but in the kitchen where he was assigned to work in the monastery. It was said of Brother Lawrence, "He was even more at one with God in his common activities, than when he turned from them for the formal activities of retreat."[4] He himself stated, "The time of busyness does not with me differ from the time of prayer, and in the noise and clatter of my kitchen. While several persons are at the same time calling for different things, I possess God in as great tranquillity as if I were upon my knees at the Blessed Sacrament."

Others noted his calm and peace in daily life. They were attracted to it and sought his counsel. How could he manage to be so undisturbed by the distractions and frustrations he encountered? How could he walk so intimately with God in a constantly busy place (the kitchen) to which, in his own words, he had "a strong natural aversion"?

Brother Lawrence had learned to make the Lord his dwelling place, and he sought never to depart from it. How? This simple monk (and I emphasize simple to remind us that he was an ordinary person like you and me, not an extraordinary spiritual leader to whom we might have some difficulty relating) wrote to a friend, "It is not needful always to be in church to be with God. We can make a chapel of our heart, to which we can from time to time withdraw to have gentle, humble, loving communion with Him." So how did he make a chapel of the heart? "I have found," he continued, "that we can establish in ourselves a sense of the presence of God by continually talking with Him."

Connect by Continually Talking with God

On the way to work when heavy traffic slows my pace. At a stoplight. Can I turn off the radio and use this time to talk with God about the day ahead? To pray for the people in their cars around me? (Perhaps they have no one to pray for them.) For the coworker who is giving me problems? For my children as they go through their day at school? For my husband, my family, my neighbors? This "prayer on the run" keeps Christ ever before us and those we care about ever before Him.

A friend keeps a list of people to pray for in her car. The paper is stuck on the dashboard for easy reference as she drives. Since the average mother today claims that she spends more time in her car than at home, this is not a bad idea to consider! It certainly would be a good way to use the time caught in a traffic jam.

Our days are filled with moments in which our hands may be occupied, but our hearts can turn to God in prayer. Not only intercessory prayer on the behalf of others but conversation about the details of our days and the concerns of our hearts. Prayer is talking with God as we talk with a friend. For the woman whose career is home and family or the one who balances a job outside the home with her family, Frank Laubach offers good advice for enjoying Christ's presence in the activities of home: "There are women who cultivate Christ's companionship while cooking, washing dishes, sweeping, serving, and caring for children. Aids which they find helpful are: whisper to the Lord about each small matter, knowing that He loves to help. Hum or sing a favorite hymn."[5]

Connect by Cultivating Christ's Companionship

A close friend comes over for a visit. You know each other well, so there's no need to be formal. She sits at the kitchen table drinking a cup of coffee while you stand at the counter, mixing together the ingredients for a cake. You talk easily, laugh together, pause for a few moments to pursue a more serious point. You chat about the things on your heart while you work.

Christ is our constant, unseen companion. It is a wonderful and amazing truth that the Lord of the universe desires to be our friend and is present to hear what is on our hearts at any moment of any day. He is present to laugh with us and cry with us, to savor the beauty of the first flowers of spring, to endure the cold winter mornings as we head out the door, to bear the burden of a difficult day.

During our first years of marriage, when Louis was in medical school and I worked with college students through InterVarsity Christian Fellowship, we lived in a tiny cottage near the edge of campus. I would often come home tired after a day filled with people, not yet ready to plunge into the work waiting in the house.

The large, black rocking chair on the old front porch beckoned. With a mug of coffee in hand, I would sit together with the Lord for a few moments. Sometimes I would talk with Him, sometimes I would just sit in His presence and enjoy being with Him, cultivating His companionship.

The Westminster Catechism expresses wonderfully this aspect of our relationship with God in its very first question posed to the church:

"What is man's chief end?"

"To glorify God and enjoy Him forever."

Note that the answer does not say our goal is to enjoy God's benefits, although we certainly do since He is gracious to bestow them freely on us. But God always has far more in mind for us than we often settle for. We are able to enjoy God Himself. Imagine how changed would be the lives of many Christians if we applied this truth! Although I certainly enjoy receiving cards and gifts from my husband, my real joy is in being with him. If he set a package at the door every day for me to open, each one full of delightful surprises, they would not substitute for his presence beside me.

I have, at other times and in other places, mentally leaned my head wearily against the Lord's shoulder and rested it there, quiet in His presence. We have laughed together on occasion over something He has done (or over some foolishness of mine!), and I have often entered into His embrace while crying. There is great joy and deep peace in knowing Christ sovereignly as Lord and intimately as friend.

Connect by Sharing Everything with God

Nothing is too small for God's concern. Not for the One who sees each sparrow that falls to the ground and who numbers the very hairs of your head. Therefore, "Do not be anxious about anything, but in everything, by prayer and petition, with thanksgiving, present your requests to God. And the peace of God, which transcends all understanding, will guard your hearts and your minds in Christ Jesus" (Phil. 4:6–7).

The peace that goes beyond all understanding is a promise to us. This peace is ours when we continually place our anxieties in God's care. And when we take them back into our own hands, as is our tendency, we simply give them over to Him again. And again, as often as we need to hand them over and keep from carrying them ourselves. I have found these verses from Philippians among the most practical in teaching me how to "sit down inside."

Thomas Kelly writes, "There is a way of life so hid with Christ in God that in the midst of the day's business one is inwardly lifting brief prayers, short ejaculations of praise, subdued whispers of adoration and tender love to the Beyond that is within. No one need know about it. . . . Walk on the streets and chat with your friends. But every moment behind the scenes be in prayer, offering yourselves in continuous obedience. I find this internal continuous prayer life absolutely essential. It can be carried on day and night, in the thick of business, in home and school."[6]

Connect by Meditating on a Favorite Hymn

The Psalms are filled with commands to sing to the Lord (Pss. 5:11; 30:4; 33:1; 47:6; 98:1 to name a few).

God delights in the joy of His people; singing expresses our joy. We are loving God when we sing to Him. It also can turn our burdened minds from what troubles us. The great hymns of the faith and modern Scripture songs remind us of biblical truths when we need them. They help us to remember, in a difficult moment, the One in control.

Many Christians are familiar with the writings of Oswald Chambers, especially *My Utmost for His Highest*. Fewer of us are familiar with his equally dedicated wife, known as Biddy, who was responsible for diligently taking shorthand notes of his many talks and compiling them after his death into the books that now challenge and bless us. David McCasland's book, *Abandoned to God*, wonderfully relates the story of Oswald Chambers's life but also reveals the character of Biddy as a woman whose heart was fully dedicated to her Lord. One incident related in the book shows her attitude in a domestic crisis:

> When the cat ate the fish Biddy had laid out for dinner and extra guests arrived unexpectedly, she searched the pantry for an alternative and sang, "Praise my soul, the King of Heaven." When everything was back to normal, she would declare it so by saying, "There we are, praise the Lord, all nice and straight again."[7]

Do you wonder, as I do, what her mind was thinking as her lips were singing? I can imagine, at least, since I have often deliberately sung "Great Is Thy Faithfulness" as a needed reminder of God's work in my life, or have called forth a Scripture song to sing God's praises in order to combat internal grumblings. Keeping a hymnal in a readily available spot or playing worship music help to turn a troubled mind to the Lord. If music soothes the savage beast, it also calms the human heart. In Biddy's case, and often in my own, it is a deliberate act of faith, a declaration of trust in God for the moments that threaten to overwhelm.

When we continually talk with God as we walk through our day, we make a chapel of our hearts and a dwelling place for our souls. We connect with our source of strength. Bringing each "small matter" before Him keeps Him before us. Singing His praises turns our hearts to His truths and lifts our minds from their burdens. By cultivating His companionship in each "place" of our lives, whether it be the office, the store, the hospital, the kitchen, or the car, we remain in the quiet center of His presence no matter where we are.

> *But as for me, it is good to be near God.*
> —Psalm 73:28

> *You will fill me with joy in your presence.*
> —Psalm 16:11

Be Still Before God

> Do as little children, who with one hand held fast by their father, and with the other gather strawberries or mulberries along the hedges: So you, gathering and managing the affairs of this world with one hand, with the other hold fast the hand of your Heavenly Father, turning yourself toward him from

time to time to see if your employments be pleas-
ing to him. And take heed above all things that you
have not let go of his hand and his protection.
                                    —St. Francis de Sales

Suggestion: Sing a love song of praise to the Lord to
begin your time with Him.

- Psalm 16:8–11
- Psalm 37:3–7, 23–24
- Psalm 73:23–26
- Psalm 27:8
- Matthew 28:20

∽

Look to the world and be distressed;
Look to yourself and be depressed;
But look to Jesus and be at rest.
                                    —Corrie ten Boom

6

Be Focused

∽

While we are looking at God we do not see ourselves—blessed riddance.[1]

—A. W. Tozer

Let us fix our eyes on Jesus, the author and
perfecter of our faith. . . .

—Hebrews 12:2

A multitude of books on management line the
shelves of bookstores and libraries. Arranging our clos-
ets, kitchen shelves, bathroom cabinets, menus, and
daily schedules should never be a problem if we will
only scan the shelf for the right self-help book. Or so
we are supposed to think! Many of the books do have
useful ideas and are worth reading. Often their suggestions are not new. The sound advice just needs to
be applied to better order our lives.

One of my favorite suggestions, perhaps because it
is so simple, is the advice given by one organized

sibling to her hopelessly messy sister. The former eyed some wet tea bags lying on the counter, left there after brewing a cup of tea, and stated matter-of-factly, "Throw away your tea bags—now." It was the moment of enlightenment for the unorganized sister. The message was simple. Clean up after yourself. Do it now and you won't have a mess later.

Organizing is essential in a woman's world today. Yet, even if we do manage to organize our outward lives, they can still seem messy at times. The most scheduled of days may be fraught with unplanned distractions. Interruptions come from outside ourselves—telephone calls, unexpected visits, emergency situations, delays.

Distractions rise from within as well. Our minds can't seem to focus on the job at hand. Our bodies feel tired or ill. Perhaps we just "wake up on the wrong side of the bed" and the day rides unproductively on an ill mood.

Maybe, despite well-ordered plans, we become overwhelmed with all there is to do. Deadlines to meet, relationships to nurture, expectations to fulfill (that others put on us and that we put on ourselves) crowd our days. I sometimes feel as if I've stepped on a fast-moving carousel and am simply hanging on as best I can for the ride. Have you felt that way? No amount of advice from management experts can stop the rush of responsibilities that sometimes spins us around. What we need at those times is to focus on internal management. We need to learn how to handle inwardly the outward moments of stress.

God offers advice for such days, to help keep our internal home in order despite the state of the external home. His advice may be as simple as throwing away the tea bags or looking to Jesus.

Focus on Jesus

We can be assured that God is looking to us. "For the eyes of the LORD move to and fro throughout the earth," His Word says, "that He may strongly support those whose heart is completely His" (2 Chron. 16:9 NASB).

Elisabeth Elliot writes of an overwhelming day in her book, *Keep a Quiet Heart*. "When Lars and I returned from a fortnight in Scotland and England there was the expected pile-up of work awaiting us and the usual temptation to feel overwhelmed by it. . . . Do you know the feeling of utter inadequacy to cope? I'm sure you do. But I believe the enemy of our souls is specially alert at such times, seeking to use them to turn us in on ourselves rather than upwards to the One who stands ready to be our Refuge and Helper."[2]

Satan gleefully stands ready to use stress to "turn us in on ourselves." Weariness, anxiety, tension, frustration, irritability, depression—all are signs that the enemy of our souls has stepped into the situation. We have let him in by keeping our eyes turned downward, by becoming overwhelmed by what we see that needs to be done, or by turning inward and reminding ourselves of our inadequacies and failures.

Jesus stands ready to be our helper. We only have to look upward to remember He is there and can enter the situation.

Elisabeth Elliot goes on to write, "In every event He seeks an entrance to my heart, yes, even in my most helpless, fruitless, futile moments. The very cracks and empty crannies of my life, my perplexities and hurts and botched-up jobs, He wants to fill with Himself, His joy, His life. The more unsatisfactory my 'performance,' the more He calls me to share His yoke. I should know by now that mine makes me tired and overburdened. He urges me to learn of Him: 'I am gentle and humble in heart. '"[3]

Focusing on Jesus has lifted my spirit and calmed my soul more than I can recount, but one moment stands out clearly. We were home on furlough and living in rented housing, a nice house graciously furnished by our church since we have little furniture and goods of our own in the States. It was wonderful having a home full of modern conveniences after three years of primitive living, and I was enjoying life in the States. As the moment of departure for our second term in Chad approached, I found myself looking longingly at the beautiful homes lining the neighborhood streets in our city. Every time I drove to the grocery store, school, or wherever an errand took me, my eyes would turn to any "For Sale" sign along the road. If I liked the house, I would continue down the street daydreaming about buying it and settling into a home of our own.

This focus on homes for sale did not help my enthusiasm about returning to pit toilets, bucket showers, and cooking over charcoal for another three years. While outwardly preparing for departure, inwardly I was frustrated and discontented. Only when the Lord gently rebuked me did the restlessness cease.

"Susan," He reminded me, "your eyes are not focused. You are looking to the things that ultimately do not matter. Look to Me and be at rest."

After this admonition from the One who knew my heart, I took each occasion of seeing a house for sale as a signal to look to Jesus and thank Him for His perfect will for our lives. By doing so, I let Him into the "cracks and crannies" of my heart that were pulling it apart. When He filled them with Himself, replacing the temporary distractions (homes for sale) with eternal perspectives, especially the privilege of serving Him wherever He chose to use me, peace returned. Sometimes in those months, the only reason I could offer for leaving life in the States and taking it up again in Chad was that I loved Jesus. Loving Him, I wanted His will above all else, even above my own desires. Deliberately looking to Him rather than to the homes that surrounded me kept my eyes "fixed on Jesus" and restored peace to my soul.

By the time we actually left for that next term, I was able to write sincerely in my journal:

> We leave this greenery for desert scrub and thorn once more, for the other terrain well-loved. I feel as if today I put back on my other self. I leave behind the woman who loves beautifully decorated homes and stylish clothes, rolling green hills and Canadian geese flying in formation for a landing on the pond. That hat, full of color and flowers, is set aside. I reach in the closet for my other hat and fix it on my head. A jaunty tilt to the brown felt of the outback, symbol of adventure and strength, perseverance and stubborn will with a large dose of humor to help one cope. I put on the hat and resolutely

fix my gaze ahead. There is no mourning for
the other woman. Both are myself and both receive their due and fully live their lives. It is a
grand and glorious way to be.

Looking to Jesus can be a spontaneous turning of
the heart heavenward in the car or it can be a more
deliberate effort.

I know a dentist who was having difficulty with a
secretary in her office. The secretary's personality irritated her constantly. Conscious of her Christian wit-
ness in the office, the dentist was desperate for a way
to handle the moments of frustration. Eventually, on
the advice of a friend to take each moment to the Lord,
she began to go into the office bathroom every time
she felt irritated. She stepped away from the situation
and turned her focus to Jesus, asking for His help, and
thanking Him for the secretary. No doubt the office
staff wondered about her frequent trips to the bathroom, but she found over time that the irritation de-
creased and she was able to be more at rest in the office.

A mother at home may need to designate her own
"time-out chair." When anger mounts, she can tell her
children she needs to be alone with Jesus for a minute.
Just watching Mom put herself into a "time-out chair"
ought to fascinate a child enough to produce momentary quiet! She can set the kitchen timer for three or
five minutes and use the time to quiet an angry heart,
to pray, to read Scripture, or simply to "count to ten"
(very slowly). Or go to another room (again, the bathroom makes a very good instant chapel where no one
questions your need to be alone!). Stepping out of the

noise and into the quiet center of His presence can put household disorder and childish behavior into perspective. Having been with Jesus, she can return to the same situation with a more restful heart and maybe some ideas on handling what chaos surrounds her.

Susannah Wesley, mother of John and Charles Wesley along with seventeen other children, had her share of stressful days. Life was not easy as a mother of so many children and as a pastor's wife who often had to labor hard, physically and emotionally, to make ends meet. She was known to throw her apron over her head when she needed time out to cope. The children learned that this was her signal for "Do not disturb."

When work mounts, rather than stepping up our pace in order to run with the load, we need actually to pull back and first bring everything before the Lord.

> *Commit to the LORD whatever you do, and your plans will succeed.*
> —Proverbs 16:3

> *Trust in the LORD with all your heart and lean not on your own understanding; in all your ways acknowledge him, and he will make your paths straight.*
> —Proverbs 3:5–6

This can be done by simply asking God to quiet your mind about the work ahead or by asking His help in ordering your day. Or it can be a more focused "management session" with the CEO of our life. Lay your schedule or "to-do" list before the Lord in prayer.

Lift each individual item to the throne of grace, and remember, "The mind of man plans his ways, but the LORD directs his steps" (Prov. 16:9 NASB).

Ask God for insights into your schedule. Keep a notepad available for any thoughts He gives during this time of prayer. Is there someone you should call or visit or send a card to? What needs special attention? What can be laid aside for the moment? How can you handle this person, this meeting, this project?

It is possible that He may ask you to whittle down your commitments. Stepping out of the marketplace of demands into a quiet place with the Lord helps us to remember priorities and put our activities into perspective. We see that some are not so pressing and can be set aside for awhile or even crossed off the list permanently. In the light of His priorities, we can examine our motives for each activity and discern whether or not we are doing them for unnecessary reasons, such as pride or guilt or a feeling that we have to be involved to prove our worth. When I am sincerely seeking to be available to the Lord, it is easier to say no to those activities which are not in His plans for my use of time without anxious concern for the opinions of others. Neither do we want to use God as an excuse for laziness or personal agendas, but we can learn to rest in our schedules by seeking His agenda rather than wearying ourselves trying to fulfill the needs and expectations of others, doing more than we should and more than He ever intended for us to do.

Looking to Jesus as the manager of our schedules develops within us a peace and certainty about our days that cannot be found in books and articles on time management.

Bringing our weekly and daily calendars before Him goes much deeper than simplifying activities. It helps us to simplify our very souls by focusing on one single goal, that is to do His will and be about His business in the world. Rather than being pulled in many directions, we are centered on one direction, and our minds are at peace. Thomas Kelly states this well:

> I have in mind something deeper than the simplification of our external programs, our absurdly crowded calendars of appointments through which so many pantingly and frantically gasp. These do become simplified in holy obedience, and the poise and peace we have been missing can really be found. But there is a deeper, an internal simplification of the whole of one's personality, stilled, tranquil, in childlike trust listening ever to Eternity's whisper, walking with a smile in the dark. This amazing simplification comes when we "center down," when life is lived with singleness of eye, from a Holy Center where the breath and stillness of Eternity are heavy upon us and we are wholly yielded to Him.[4]

Committing the daily schedule, the business project, or the week ahead to His guidance brings an eternal perspective to our activities. We also remember that God is in control, even of the interruptions and the difficulties we face. The telephone call that interrupts my project and changes the course of my day, sending all plans awry, must be seen not as an accident of fate to frustrate, but as an instrument of God to serve His purposes in my life.

Hannah Whitall Smith considered the people who interrupted her schedule or who were difficult to bear as the "bottles" that hold our spiritual medicine, but she considered it the Father's loving hand of love that poured out the medicine.[5] She saw beyond her difficulties to the One who was ultimately in control.

We have the example of Janet Erskine Stuart, who delighted in seeing her plan upset by unexplained events, saying that it gave her great comfort, and that she looked on such things as an assurance that God was watching over her stewardship, securing the accomplishment of His will, and working out His own designs. Whether she traced the secondary causes to the prayer of a child, to the imperfection of an individual, to obstacles arising from misunderstandings, or to interference of outside agencies, she was joyfully and graciously ready to recognize God's ruling hand, and to allow herself to be guided by it.[6]

Louis and I have had our share of difficult moments, constant interruptions, and demanding people as we have served in Chad. There were times when we were so weary that if there had been a plane to land in our bush town, we would have been on it when it left! Thankfully, a plane never landed on the dirt airstrip at any of those times and we came through them to a place of joy before one actually arrived. We have learned, instead of running from the difficulties, to find God's stamp on them, to believe, as Hannah Whitall Smith wrote, that His loving hand is somehow behind them all.

Looking to Jesus in moments of difficulty reminds us

that He is involved. Nothing has slipped by without His awareness. "Nothing," advised Mrs. Smith, "can disturb or harm us except He shall see that it is best for us and shall stand aside to let it pass." Knowing that God is in everything, we can ask Him what we are to learn. We can thank Him in faith for His perfect plan, even if it seems imperfect to us at the moment.

Taking time out of a difficult situation to look to Christ reminds us of His presence and His truths. We are reminded of His enabling power in a situation that seems overwhelming. We return to what really matters in life and regain right priorities. We are reminded of His love and so are lifted out of depression. His peace replaces tension and uncertainty. His grace replaces irritation. His wisdom replaces confusion.

We may need to deliberately look to Jesus again and again until an issue is resolved. No matter how often we must come to Him with the same situation, we can rest assured that Jesus is ever ready to hear and to help.

Be Still Before God

Suggestion: Choose a short prayer, even a prayer phrase, to say to the Lord throughout the day as a reminder of His presence. Examples from the spiritual classics are:

Lord, have mercy on me.

Not my will but Thy will be done.

Help me, Lord, to do Your will.

I love You, Lord. Help me to hear Your voice.

- Psalm 25:15
- Psalm 123:2
- Hebrews 12:1–2
- Psalm 121:1–4
- Psalm 141:8

＿＿

From prayer that asks that I may be
Sheltered from winds that beat on Thee,
From fearing when I should aspire,
From faltering when I should climb higher,
From silken self, O captain, free
Thy soldier who would follow Thee.

From subtle love of softening things,
From easy choices, weakenings,
Not thus are spirits fortified,
Not this way went the Crucified;
From all that dims Thy Calvary,
O Lamb of God, deliver me.

Give me the love that leads the way,
The faith that nothing can dismay,
The hope no disappointments tire,
The passion that will burn like fire.
Let me not sink to be a clod,
Make me Thy fuel, O Flame of God.

　　　　　　　　　　—Amy Carmichael (1867–1951)

7

Be Trusting

❧

Peace does not dwell in outward things, but in
the heart prepared to wait trustfully and quietly
on Him who has all things safely in His hands.[1]
—Elisabeth Elliot

*You will keep in perfect peace him whose mind
is steadfast, because he trusts in you.*
—Isaiah 26:3

The story is told of an amazing feat that took place
at Niagara Falls in the nineteenth century. A French
acrobat named Bondin claimed he could cross Niagara
Falls on a tightrope. On the day of this performance, a
large crowd gathered, curious to see such an exhibi-
tion of bravery or foolhardiness, depending on what
view each observer took of his claim. With all eyes on
him, the Frenchman mounted the rope, balanced his
pole, and slowly walked 1,100 feet across the Falls
while the water crashed and surged violently 160 feet

below him. When he safely reached the other side, the crowd cheered wildly and even the skeptics pounded each other on the back in delight at what they had just witnessed.

But the acrobat wasn't through with his performance. He motioned the cheering crowd back to silence. The onlookers watched in quiet awe as he took hold of a wheelbarrow and proceeded to retrace his steps, this time walking the rope while pushing a wheelbarrow before him. Again the water pounded below as he stepped slowly along the wire, one foot placed carefully before the other, eyes ahead, and hands firmly balancing the wheelbarrow. When he reached the ground on the other side, the crowd burst into a frenzy of applause. One man ran through the crowd to his side, grabbed his arm, and yelled in exultation, "I knew you could do it! I believed so much you could do it that I bet my entire savings on that fact!" The Frenchman smiled and looked at the excited man standing beside him. "Good," he said, "You're just the person I need. Get in the wheelbarrow and I will take you back across."

The story never tells of a third walk across the Falls. That's because the man in the crowd never accepted Bondin's offer. His faith couldn't go that far. He had great faith in the acrobat's ability to do something incredible, faith enough even to bet his personal resources, but not faith enough to get in the wheelbarrow himself. Who would blame him? I certainly don't! I imagine that after seeing the man's face turn pale at the suggestion, the Frenchman had mercy on him and laughed, assuring him that such a step wasn't necessary.

We ourselves can be very much like the man who ran through the crowd. We do believe in God. We believe enough to stake resources of time and money, energy and emotions, on the fact that He exists and is at work in the world. But when it comes to the things that matter dearly to us (in the man's case, his life), we are hesitant to trust God so completely. Always before us is the question, "What if . . . ?"

The man at the falls believed and witnessed the acrobat's competence, but as for putting his own life on the line, he wondered "What if I fall? What if this time he doesn't make it?" He was willing to go only so far in believing. And so are many of us, despite all of our claims of faith.

As long as there is some doubt, we will not be able to fully trust. As long as we are not able to trust, we will not be able to fully rest. Have you written a check when the checkbook hasn't been balanced in a while? You write the check anyway, hoping that there's enough money to cover it, but you do so with an uneasy mind. Only if you know a sufficient amount is actually in the bank can you hand the check over with a peaceful mind.

I have stated this point previously, but because it is the foundation for our knowing true peace, it can never be stated enough. We are not able to rest until we trust. We are not able to experience true peace until we fully trust God.

What kind of trust do we need? Elisabeth Elliot writes in her book *All That Ever Was Ours*, "The usual notion of hope is a particular outcome: physical healing, for example. The Christian notion on the other hand, is a manner of life. . . . I am held by the confidence of God's trustworthiness."[2] Her distinction between the "usual notion of hope" and Christian hope is significant. Which one we apply in our lives makes the difference between uncertainty and peace. The first hope perches on the phrase, "What if . . ." and depends on a certain outcome, receiving what we ask. The second hope is in God Himself and rests on the words, "Even so . . . ," not because we cease expecting Him to give what we ask, but because we trust utterly in His wisdom to give what is best. This is the kind of trust we need in order to know true peace. It means an exchange of our "What if . . ." for an "Even so, Lord."

In Chad we enjoy going camping as a family. This seems odd to the Chadians who know us, because they live a camping lifestyle. We do as well, even in our own home, since no running water means we must shower daily from a bucket of water and use a pit toilet. But still we love, at times, to drive further into the bush, select a spot that is unlikely to be invaded by curious village boys, and spend a night camping. These outings provide uninterrupted private time as a family, something we cherish in the highly sociable African culture.

On one such excursion we found an isolated spot situated between two high mountains of rock. We parked our vehicle as far in the opening of the rocks as possible and set up camp. We had brought two chickens to roast for supper, but as there are no grocery stores in our town to provide nicely packaged meats, the chickens we brought were alive. They needed to be slaughtered, plucked, and cleaned before being put on the spit over the fire. Our son, relishing the opportunity to show his scouting skills, reached for the cardboard box that housed our dinner. The chickens, however, were not so agreeable to his intentions and both escaped the minute he lifted them from the box. We spent an hour chasing two frantic hens and finally retrieved them after many scratches and bruises. They succumbed to their fate, Scott did a fine job of roasting them over the fire, and we had a wonderful meal under the stars.

During the chase, however, I happened to stand upon a flat rock that projected over a large opening in the ground. Peering into the opening, I started back in surprise. Stretched across the length of the opening was a snakeskin, a very long snakeskin. It was the largest I had ever seen, and there it was, lying close to our campground. Needless to say, my first thought was to the snake that had shed this monster of a skin. I called Louis over, then the children, and we finally agreed that seeing the skin did not necessarily mean we would see the snake. We named the owner of the skin "Big John" and went on preparing supper.

My thoughts turned to Big John constantly throughout the evening but we never saw him, probably because he wasn't there. The night that followed, however, was long and restless. I could not sleep easily knowing that Big John might still be living under that rock and at any moment might decide to visit us. I tossed and turned and listened for sounds of swishing in the night. The following morning, seeking company in misery, I asked the children how they slept.

"Fine," they all replied.

"Fine? You didn't have a hard time sleeping because of the snake?"

"No," they said calmly, "We knew that you and Dad would take care of us."

And that was that.

I smiled at their faith in us, although the thought of having to protect them against a seven-foot snake was daunting. (The length of the snake is no exaggeration. We lifted the skin out of the hole the next day and measured it.) The children's confidence in our care, however, reminded me of how my faith in God should be. Uncomplicated, trusting, and sure. "We knew you would take care of us."

Our three children trusted in us. The snakeskin remained, along with the possibility of a visit from its owner, but they slept because they trusted us to take care of them.

Can we rest so fully in the Lord? Can we sleep peacefully because we trust in God's ability to take care of us? When I become anxious, tense, or fretful, I ask myself, "Apart from all the church talk that flows so easily from my lips, deep down in my heart, what do I really believe about God?" Do I believe He can do great things, like the acrobat, yet when it comes to something that matters greatly in my life, do I hold back from trusting He can carry me through? God asks us to have a "get in the wheelbarrow" trust, a faith that abandons itself wholly to His care. He asks us to have the uncomplicated faith of a child. He asks us to look, not to a possible outcome, but to Him.

The essential question is, "What do I really believe about God?"

Is He who He says He is? Is His Word true? When I read a promise in Scripture, do I believe it is true in any situation? Do I take God at His Word?

The missionary life provides ample opportunities to trust God. With the absence of many comforts and conveniences, Louis and I turn to Him often for our spiritual, emotional, and physical needs. Our days can be draining spiritually as we are asked to persevere when little fruit is evident from evangelistic efforts. Temperatures that reach 120 degrees, illnesses that result from living in primitive conditions, a constant outpouring of energy, all drain us physically. We become drained emotionally from a lack of privacy and from constant exposure to the poverty and pain of those whom God has called us to serve. Lacking the dynamic church services, Bible studies, and fellowship one finds in the States, we can easily be drained spiritually. We could not continue in this ministry if we did not trust fully in the One who called us.

When the task is particularly overwhelming or the difficulties threaten to outweigh the privileges of missionary service, we are tempted to ask, "Why must You let it be so hard, Lord?" Then we are encouraged by His Word found in Psalm 25:10: "All the paths of the LORD are lovingkindness and truth" (NASB). And we are challenged to believe that if His Word is true, then it is true even in our most difficult circumstances.

Early in our missionary career, the writings of Amy Carmichael, the missionary to India who saved countless children from lives of prostitution, encouraged us to take God at His Word. We have practically memorized her commentary on Psalm 25:10. She wrote:

I have pondered this verse lately, and have found that it feeds my spirit. All does not mean "all—except the paths I am walking in now," or "nearly all—except this especially difficult and painful path." All must mean all. So your path with its unexplained sorrow or turmoil, and mine with its sharp flints and briars—and both of our paths, with their unexplained perplexities, their sheer mystery—they are His paths, on which He will show Himself loving and faithful. Nothing else; nothing less.[3]

Now, when Louis and I find ourselves in especially difficult or irritating circumstances, we look at each other and quote, "All means all." Do we believe it? Yes, we do, because we have come to know the One who promised it, and we have come to see that, indeed, all of His paths are undergirded by His lovingkindness and His truth.

Another favorite verse of mine is Isaiah 26:3: "The steadfast of mind Thou wilt keep in perfect peace, because he trusts in Thee" (NASB). I used to read this verse in frustration, because although I was working on taking God at His Word, I was far from experiencing perfect peace. "OK, God, here it is," I would say to Him. "Your Word says that You will keep me in perfect peace. So why isn't it happening if You promised it?" One day I realized that within the verse itself was my answer, and it was twofold.

If I am to experience God's perfect peace, I have my own part to fulfill. I must have a steadfast mind, that is, a mind stayed on Christ (looking to Jesus) and a trusting heart ("Even so, Lord"). A mind stayed on Christ plus a heart that trusts in Him equals this perfect peace.

Not just every once in a while, when I'm feeling good or when the problems are minimal enough to see a resolution, but steadfastly, perseveringly, confidently, even when there appears to be no hope.

This is the kind of unwavering trust that springs throughout the centuries from the lips of martyrs and saints in the church.

It is the kind of trust that enabled the sixteenth-century Reformer, John Bradford, to encourage nineteen-year-old John Leaf before both were martyred for their faith. It enabled him to speak the cheering words as they were about to be burned at the stake, "Be of good comfort, brother; for we shall have a merry supper with the Lord this night!"[4]

It is the kind of trust that enabled Susannah Spurgeon, wife of the great preacher, Charles Haddon Spurgeon, to exclaim during a time of painful illness, "When the fire of affliction draws songs of praise from us, then indeed are we purified, and our God is glorified. Singing in the fire! Yes! God helping us, if that is the only way to get harmony out of these hard, apathetic hearts, let the furnace be heated seven times more."[5]

It is the kind of trust that enabled Corrie ten Boom to write from her solitary confinement cell in a concentration camp during World War II, "Please never worry about me; sometimes it may be dark, but the Savior provides His light and how wonderful that is," and from another cell in yet another camp, "God knows the way; we are at peace with everything."[6]

It is the kind of trust that sustained Rosalind Goforth as a pioneer missionary to China with her husband,

Jonathan Goforth (who himself has been called China's most outstanding evangelist). During their years of missionary service, Rosalind and her husband endured sufferings that many of us can hardly imagine. One account of their life describes when Jonathan "lay bleeding after having been hacked in the back, neck, and head with a sword. He thought surely he would be the next of the dozens of China missionaries to be killed during the Boxer Rebellion of 1900. But miraculously he survived."[7] The final result of their sufferings was not always so positive. They buried five of their eleven children on Chinese soil. Even so, Rosalind could write in her book *How I Know . . . God Answers Prayer:*

> It is so true that
> We may trust Him wholly
>   all for us to do;
> Those who trust Him wholly
>   find Him wholly true.[8]

True? When the result of obedience is the loss of five children? When trusting God to guide you in the right path leads you to a concentration camp?

Yes, when the kind of trust that finds God to be wholly true in any situation is based not on circumstances nor on outcomes, but on His character. When we take God at His Word, when we are "held by the confidence of God's trustworthiness" rather than by the hope of certain outcomes, when we turn our "What if . . ." into an "Even so . . . ," then we can echo Rosalind Goforth's words in reflecting on her life, "It can all be summed up in one word: resting."[9]

Be Still Before God

> If I wonder why something trying is allowed, and press for prayer that it may be removed; if I cannot be trusted with any disappointment, and cannot go on in peace under any mystery, then I know nothing of Calvary love.[10]
>
> —Amy Carmichael

Suggestion: Write a poem or hymn of trust to the Lord. We cannot fully rest in the Lord until we fully trust Him. How do we gain peace, according to these verses? What is required of us as we seek to put our trust in the Lord?

- Isaiah 26:3–4
- Colossians 3:12–17
- Philippians 4:6–7
- Matthew 6:25–34

Consider these questions before the Lord:

- How do you handle the times when you feel disappointed by God, when prayers are not answered or when He seems to be silent even when you are sincerely seeking Him?
- In what areas of your life do you find it most difficult to trust God and let Him have control?
- What are the areas in your life now for which you need to trust God?

∽

There is joy, joy found nowhere else,
When we can look up into Christ's face
When he says,
"Am I not enough for thee, Mine own?"
With a true, "Yes, Lord, thou art enough."[11]
                                        —Amy Carmichael

8

Be Willing

∽

Lord, loosen in me the hold of visible things.
—George MacDonald

Trust in him at all times, O people.
—Psalm 62:8

$\mathcal{I}$ want to take you with me on another journey. This journey began over twenty years ago on the college campus when God challenged me to be willing to rearrange my priorities in life. This challenge meant, for me, to look beyond my immediate world of family, friends, and studies in order to see His world, to have on my heart what is on His heart, the redemption of the world He created and loves. This meant, I knew, a willingness to be involved in missions, perhaps even to become a missionary myself. At the same time and in the same way, God was challenging a premed student who happened to be in the same campus fellowship as I. So when our relationship grew beyond friendship and Louis and I knew we wanted to spend our lives together, we also knew that meant perhaps serving together somewhere in the world as missionaries.

The years that followed our wedding, however, were busy enough to keep the possibility of a missionary career on the shelf. They were spent in medical school and residency for Louis, pursuing graduate studies in Bible for both of us, and welcoming the birth of three children. We became involved in a church, worked with the junior high youth group, began a Bible study, made many dear friends, and settled into a fulfilling family and church life in the States.

There came the point, however, when we were finished with our studies, medical and biblical, and realized we were finally free to go overseas if we wanted to. But years after that initial desire to be involved in missions, did we still want to? Louis had been asked to join the faculty of his residency program and found he thoroughly enjoyed teaching. This was something he would be happy to do as a career. We would be giving up quite a lot by leaving our life in the States, where we could certainly serve Him. Friends and family reminded us that there are still many needs in America. But God had put His heart for the world on our hearts, and He had stamped us with the seal, "You are not your own; you were bought at a price" (1 Cor. 6:19–20). We had given our lives to Christ years ago, and that meant we belonged to Him. Our joy and purpose in life came from doing His will, not from pursuing our own. We could not remain home if He wanted us to serve Him elsewhere.

We also realized that any motivation for a missionary life of our own making would not endure under pressure. By now we had made two short-term mission trips and reality had set in. The missionary life is not an easy one. We could see that clearly in only a few months of experience. If, after two months in a challenging setting, we were ready to come home, what would be our response when we faced such a difficult lifestyle over a period of years? We knew that an adventurous spirit, a desire to "do good" in the world, even an affinity for camping would all give way quickly after idealism wore off. Only the sure knowledge that we were in the center of God's will would last.

In order to make the decision, we packed the children off to their grandparents and headed to the mountains for a weekend. Another couple, dear friends in the Lord, came with us, committing themselves to pray throughout the weekend as we sought God's will for our future. During that weekend of Bible study and prayer, God did indeed make clear to us that He was calling us to be missionaries. And He gave me Isaiah 42:6 as a promise: "I am the LORD, I have called you in righteousness. I will also hold you by the hand and watch over you" (NASB).

I remember the moment when I knew God was saying we were to go. I stepped outside the old, family mountain house where we were staying and stood in the darkness. As I looked up into the starry sky, so vast and wide like the world God was calling me into, tears began streaming down my face. Not because I no longer wanted to become a missionary (the desire had remained throughout the years, however dormant at times), but because I realized this was the real thing. The missionary life was no longer an interesting possibility for the future but a certainty for the here and now. God was indeed asking me to let go of the life we knew for the life He wanted us to live.

I lifted my arms and spread out my hands, palms upward as a symbol of letting go. "Yes, Lord," I said to His will for my life.

That was the first step of the journey—trusting God to know what was best for my life and being willing to follow His leading.

The second step came when we joined our mission, WEC International. This step involved our children, who were then four and two years old.

I will never forget one afternoon at our mission headquarters in Fort Washington, Pennsylvania. We were living at WEC headquarters for four months of training to become missionaries. Part of the training program was to write a research paper on the country of our calling, which by then we knew was Chad, Africa. Louis and I divided the responsibility for the paper. He researched Islam while I researched the history of Chad. It might have been better if we had switched our responsibilities. What I found wasn't easy for a mother of young children to swallow. I read article after article about famine, war, and rebel activity. The country was unstable, impoverished, and, at that time, politically dangerous. What, I thought, are we doing taking our children to this place?

One afternoon, the research was more than I could bear. I left the library early and found Scott, Susan, and Elizabeth in the nursery where they were being cared for as I studied. Their happy shouts of greeting when they saw me pierced my heart, and I wondered even more what we were doing taking them to a country like Chad. We made our way slowly up the stairs to our second-floor apartment, and I settled them down for a rest. Then I dragged myself into the adjoining living room. Feeling numb, I knelt down by a large, stuffed armchair, and cried. The tears once more streamed down my face as I thought about this African country and agonized over the life ahead for our children.

Finally my tears were exhausted, and I knelt silently, unable to speak or think. The Lord spoke gently into the silence.

"Susan," He said, "don't you know that I love your children more than you do?"

I looked up and let the words sink in. Did I believe them? Did God love my children even more than I did? Then He would know very well what He was doing if He sent them to a country like Chad. I realized that in my agony and doubts I had left Him completely out of the picture. I bowed my head in the quiet and opened my hands yet a second time.

"Yes, Lord," I said, "I do know."

At that moment, I knew I was willing to trust God. I had to let go of my children. I was to trust Him to care for them. He reminded me that afternoon that He leaves nothing out of the picture. If He calls Louis and me to be missionaries, He hasn't forgotten that our children need to come along as well. His will for us is His will for them. I can trust Him not only for my own life but also for theirs.

The third area requiring trust touched on my personal desires and tastes. It was a lesson in learning to be content, and the training ground was in Belgium.

With God's call to serve in Chad came the need to learn French, since Chad is a former French colony. We left our missionary training in Fort Washington, Pennsylvania, to spend one and a half years in Belgium studying French and, for Louis, tropical medicine at the Institute of Tropical Medicine in Antwerp. We lived in an old apartment building in an even older section of Brussels.

The building was dark and dingy with no elevators, and we lived on the third floor. You can imagine how it was to climb three flights of stairs with three young children, especially after a tiring day in the park or with a load of groceries in my arms. Those were not moments to inspire joy in a mother's heart. The apartment itself was in need of a makeover, but we didn't have extra funds to redecorate. Paint peeled on the walls. The shower, a portable type, was installed on some boards in the kitchen. Although we had many wonderful times as a family during those years of language study, exploring Brussels, living in Europe, and making many friends in the French-speaking church we attended, I began them with great dissatisfaction. I rarely mentioned it, but God knew the state of my heart.

One day I was in a particularly grumbling state over the apartment. I happened to be cleaning the bathroom, which was located at the bottom of a landing. The bathroom was all ours; we didn't have to share it with either of the families who lived below us, but we did have to leave our apartment and go down several steps to reach it. I was cleaning the window that opened to a view of the brick wall of the building next door and feeling sorry for myself. No tears this time, but there was just enough murmuring to have kept the Israelites company in the wilderness. Somewhere along the way, however, I must have ceased my inner complaints long enough for the Lord to get in a word.

"Susan," He seemed to say as I was wiping the windows, "don't you like what I gave you?"

That question made me pause in my work, and I thought about it. It didn't take me long to answer. My honest reply was, "No, Lord, I don't!"

Thankfully, God is big enough to handle our honesty, and His self-esteem remains intact no matter how we feel about Him. At the moment, I wasn't inclined to be thankful for or accepting of His choices for my life.

But His words sank into my heart. As I reflected on them, I realized what He wanted me to know. We were not living in this apartment by accident. It was, in fact, His chosen place for us at this moment in our lives. He reminded me in that tiny bathroom that His perfect and good will for me included this less than desirable dwelling, because He had lessons to teach me that couldn't be learned elsewhere—lessons of contentment, lessons of finding joy, not in my external environment or in material things, but in Him.

So eventually I prayed, "Lord, sometimes I really don't like what You're doing in my life or what You've chosen for me, but I trust You to give only what is best. It is the right place for me, and I thank You for it."

After letting go of my complaints and interior decorating desires, peace flooded my heart once again. Because I began to focus less on the things around me for my source of contentment and joy, I was able to look more to the Lord Himself. Remembering a quote from some years past, I wrote it on a piece of paper to keep in my Bible:

"I used to think God was important in my life, until I learned that He is enough."

There is a vast difference between God being important to us, and God being enough. He wanted to teach me to be satisfied with Himself and with all that He chooses for me, so He put me in that still old and drab but now dear apartment in Belgium.

The lesson of living life with trust continues as Louis and I must once again let go of our children. They are now teenagers and we can no longer provide the education or social life they need by homeschooling in a rural bush town in Africa. The hard decision was made to let them go to a boarding school, and it took a year for me to agree with God that He knew what He was doing this time. I argued with Him that it would be better for us to leave the mission field and return to the States for the educational needs of our children. But He would not give us permission to return. He made it clear that there was work yet to do in Chad and that His will for us was to continue as missionaries, even if this meant being separated for months at a time as a family.

Again the issue was trust. Was I willing to believe that God knew far better than I what was best for our children? Was I willing to believe that He loves them and has their best interests at heart? This decision concerning our children was even harder than the first one, because God was not only asking us to let them go emotionally, He was asking us to let them go physically. But God had been preparing us, for He had already taught us many lessons in the school of trust, and we had developed the habit of saying, "Yes, Lord." I was able eventually to trust the children to His care, and to write the following words to our friends and family at home:

> We believe that this is God's will for our family, and because we know God we trust fully that His will is right and good, better than any we could ever plan for ourselves. The fact that Susan, Scott, and Elizabeth are very positive about heading off to boarding school helps a great deal. (In fact, their main concern at this point is that they think I will miss them too much, not the other way around!)
>
> Sigh . . . still, it's not easy on a mother's heart.
>
> Some of you may be wondering how we can send the children away to school. Well, I'll tell you . . . " 'tain't easy." But then Jesus never said our life of faith would be easy. (That's one of those oft-quoted truths that are easier said than lived by. We don't mind saying it, but if the truth be known, we really would rather He make life easy for us than hard.)
>
> In this search for His will for our family, I have had to learn more fully what Jesus means when He says that if we want to come after Him, we

must take up our cross, deny ourselves, and follow Him (Luke 9:23). Dying to self sounds very
spiritual on paper but feels decidedly unspiritual
in the learning. Have you noticed? It has not been
easy to let go of my ideas and desires. God has
been more gracious in the process than I have
been. He has patiently brought me to yet another
level of trust. And He has taught me again that
although denying oneself and taking up one's
cross seem negative (and they are not easy paths
to tread), they do lead the way to one glorious
positive—following Him.

A noticeable element of this struggle was my
lack of joy. Joy in Christ and delight in His will
became lost in the forest of questions and
doubts. That joy was restored as the forest was
cleared and I could once more look up to see
Him and be reminded just who it is that I am
following—One who is worthy of my trust.

There is nothing, absolutely nothing greater
than living life fully for Christ. A life lived His
way will not always be easy, but it will always
be worth any cost along the way.

Be Still Before God
"Like a River Glorious," by Frances Ridley Havergal:

Like a river glorious is God's perfect peace,
Over all victorious in its bright increase;
Perfect, yet it floweth fuller ev'ry day,
Perfect, yet it groweth deeper all the way.

Hidden in the hollow of His blessed hand,
Never foe can follow, never traitor stand;
Not a surge of worry, not a shade of care,
Not a blast of hurry touch the spirit there.

Ev'ry joy or trial falleth from above,
Traced upon our dial by the Sun of Love;
We may trust Him fully all for us to do—
Those who trust Him wholly find Him wholly
    true.

By His grace, we will be able to live our lives with
open hands and sing with certainty the hymn's confident refrain:

Stayed upon Jehovah, hearts are fully blest—
Finding, as He promised, perfect peace and rest.

Suggestion: Use biblical images as you pray about
the people and circumstances that cause you anxiety.

One image is of open hands, which symbolizes letting go. As you pray, lift open hands to the Lord and
relinquish your concern or desire to control a situation and trust His greater wisdom.

Another helpful image is of the cross. Mentally place
at the foot of the cross whatever is on your heart (loved
ones, a work situation, a difficult decision, an unful-
filled desire). Leave the concern at the foot of the cross
and back away. Go to the cross again and again whenever you want to take the burden or concern back into
your own hands.

Reflect on Psalm 62, which is entitled "A Song of Trust in God Alone."

∾

I heard once of a discontented, complaining man who, to the great surprise of his friends, became bright, and happy, and full of thanksgiving. After watching him for a little while, and being convinced that the change was permanent, they asked him what had happened. "Oh," he replied, "I have changed my residence. I used to live on Grumbling Lane, but now I have moved into Thanksgiving Square, and I find that I am so rich in blessings that I am always happy." Shall we each one make this move now?[1]

—Hannah Whitall Smith

9

Resting in What We Have

⤜⤏

If thou consider the worth of the Giver, no gift will seem little, or of too mean esteem. For that cannot be little which is given by the Most High God.[1]
—Thomas à Kempis

Give thanks in all circumstances, for this is God's will for you in Christ Jesus.
—1 Thessalonians 5:18

There is a remarkable plant which grows in Chad. The French name for this plant is *Pied d'Elephant* (Elephant Foot), and it is well-named, for its thick, gray stump, with a little imagination, does resemble an elephant's foot. Our family prefers, however, to use its colloquial name, the desert rose.

The desert rose is remarkable because it grows in such unlikely places. Asserting an independent nature, it shuns the more fertile grounds needed by other plants and grows instead between clumps of rock. The plant thrives in harsh surroundings.

The desert rose is also interesting because it blooms at unlikely times. With a thick base topped by a head of bare, stubby branches, it remains stark and gray for most of the year. Even during the rainy season, it remains bare. At some point during the dry season, however, when all other plants are withering or dying, this plant blossoms. It sprouts an array of pink flowers, displaying its delicate glory in vivid contrast to the bleak landscape that surrounds it.

Whenever our family travels the sandy bush roads between towns, we love to spot the desert rose in bloom. But true to its independent nature, it grows singly, not in a group. So one can easily miss a lone plant in passing. If we are to find one, we must consciously look for it. If, however, we forget to look and focus instead on the larger landscape or on the road itself, we miss the moment of beauty in the desert as we rumble by in our car.

This desert plant provides a lesson, not only for finding a splash of color in the bleak surroundings of a sub-Saharan dry season, but also for finding peace in the larger arena of life. The lesson from the desert is clear: It matters very much where we are looking.

People often ask, after hearing us describe the primitive conditions of our life in Chad, "How can you do what you do? How can you live in such a harsh environment for years at a time and find contentment, and even joy in such a place?" We answer with our lesson from the flower. We can do what we do in Chad because we have learned to look for the desert rose. We have learned, that is, to focus on the good in our lives and to find the blessings that spring from the hard places. This strengthens our faith. This enhances our quiet center.

In Chad, we can miss the good that sustains us if we focus on the poverty, the heat and dust storms, or the needs that face us daily. If our eyes focus on our circumstances, then we grow weary and our strength fails. If our eyes focus on what we lack rather than on what we have, then we grow discontented.

Just as we miss the desert rose if we're not looking for it in our travels, we miss the blessings, the good things provided by God, unless we're looking for them. When we focus on the outward blessings in our lives, we experience a change inwardly. We become more positive and more at peace. We develop a thankful spirit and find that we can be satisfied in even the most difficult of places.

Be Thankful

One sign of a quiet center is an attitude of thankfulness. A thankful heart and mind are among God's most useful tools for rooting out discontent, grumbling, and even bitterness. Developing an attitude of thankfulness is not simply a matter of positive thinking. It is a matter of obedience, since for the Christian, giving thanks is a command, not an option. The New Testament is clear in its instruction:

> Give thanks in all circumstances, *for this is*
> *God's will for you in Christ Jesus.*
> —1 Thessalonians 5:18 (*emphasis mine*)

. . . always giving thanks to God the Father for
everything, in the name of our Lord Jesus
Christ.

—Ephesians 5:20

And whatever you do, whether in word or deed,
do it all in the name of the Lord Jesus, giving
thanks to God the Father through him.

—Colossians 3:17

The habit of giving thanks is threaded throughout the Old Testament psalms:

Give thanks to the LORD, for he is good; his love
endures forever.

—Psalms 106:1; 107:1; 118:1

We give thanks to you, O God, we give thanks,
for your Name is near; men tell of your
wonderful deeds.

—Psalm 75:1

Enter his gates with thanksgiving and his
courts with praise; give thanks to him and
praise his name.

—Psalm 100:4

David's prayer of praise for God's mercies to Israel begins with an exhortation to God's chosen people to give thanks. "Give thanks to the LORD, call on his name . . ." David commands (1 Chron. 16:8). He ends the prayer with the same call, "Give thanks to the LORD, for he is good" (16:34). David goes on to declare that Israel was called out from the nations for a purpose. What was that purpose? "That we may give thanks to your holy name, that we may glory in your praise" (16:35).

We are also God's people, called to belong to Him and, in belonging to Him, called to be different from the world around us. Part of that calling is to be thankful, which will certainly help to set us apart from the world.

A friend and I were discussing her teenage daughter who, despite the efforts her parents made to help her in a certain situation, was continually dissatisfied. My friend shook her head and sighed. "No matter what we do," she said, "it's never enough." I cringed inwardly at her words. How often, I wondered, might God rightly say the same about me? Rather than remembering what He has done and giving thanks for the many blessings He has already bestowed, I look around for what I still want and am dissatisfied. No wonder joy and peace are lacking at those times in my life!

Grumblings, complaints, and discontent are alive and well in our prosperous society, and they are joy-breakers. Giving thanks is a joy-maker. The practice of thanksgiving leads to rest and peace.

Why, then, is thanksgiving not practiced more? One problem, I imagine, is that being thankful does not always come naturally. Not everyone is an optimist by nature. Giving thanks, then, must become a deliberate choice.

Several years ago I was sitting in the kitchen of an older Christian woman as she spoke honestly about her husband and her son. She had been married long enough and had been a mother long enough to know everything possible that was imperfect about the men in her life. This knowledge, she told me with a wry smile, had begun to destroy her peace and threatened to destroy their home.

This wise woman realized her attitude of fault-finding and discontent was creating an atmosphere in the home far from what God intended. She also realized that her husband and son were not going to change, at least as fully as she would like. So she determined to change her attitude toward them. To do so, she told me, she took two pieces of paper, one for her husband and one for her son. On one paper she listed ten good qualities of her husband, and on the other, ten good qualities of her son. She then posted these two lists in her kitchen where she spent most of her day. Whenever she was tempted to complain about either her husband or her son, she would look at the appropriate list and remember their worth. As she read and remembered, she could genuinely give God thanks for these two men in her life.

She had discovered that it mattered very much where she was looking. By deliberately focusing on the positives, she was able to battle the negatives and was reminded that she was blessed indeed.

Why does God place such value on giving thanks? Perhaps because, having created us, He knows well the human psyche. He knows what we need to still our restless, driven spirits, so He commands us to give thanks for our own good. But there is a reason for thanksgiving which gives glory to God. When we choose to give thanks in the midst of difficult circumstances, we show God that we trust Him. When we lay aside our desires or grievances and choose instead to praise Him, we delight His heart.

Be Satisfied

Another sign of a quiet center is an attitude of being satisfied with what we have. A wise African pastor once told Louis and me that one can always find the negatives in life. The challenge, he said, is to look for the good. We were newly arrived on the mission field, so we took his words to heart, but they were not always easy to follow.

What if, as it seems at times, there is nothing obviously good before us? What if we can find nothing in our circumstances for which we can be thankful? Then we look beyond our circumstances to the One who controls them.

I felt this way one afternoon during our second term as missionaries. A dust storm had just rolled in, settling a fine layer of grit on everything in the house. Louis was lying on the bed ill with a stomach virus which he had caught during a recent bush trip to one of his health clinics and the children were hot, restless, and grumpy. I was tired from the morning's stream of activities and in no mood to drum up positive reasons for our family being in a mud-and-thatch town in the middle of the Chadian bush. Carrying a bucket of guava and mango peelings from the day's lunch, I trudged toward the large pit in the backyard. Frustration, mixed with a deep weariness from the day, washed over me and I turned to the Lord. Standing by the compost hole, I asked, "Lord, really, what is there to be thankful for?" I waited, and He quietly replied to my heart, "You can be thankful for Me."

I sighed, but I had to smile. God wasn't going to let me get away with self-pity, and He was right. In the dark tunnel of my grumblings, I had lost sight of an important truth: There is always the Lord, and He is enough.

If the blessings don't abound, then we look to God as the only blessing we need. When we learn to do this, we will indeed find rest for our souls.

The life of Edward Payson provides a challenging example of a soul at rest despite circumstances. Payson was a New England pastor who ministered in the early nineteenth century and was known for his powerful prayers and sermons. A friend wrote of him, "When he spread forth his hands to God, heaven seemed to come down to earth." But this man's dynamic ministry was cut short by a crippling illness that led to his early death. Even in the last stages of his illness, however, when he was in acute pain, he was able to say to a young Christian:

> Christians might avoid much trouble and inconvenience if they would only believe what they profess: that God is able to make them happy without anything else. . . . To mention my own case—God has been depriving me of one blessing after another; but as every one was removed, he has come in and filled up the place; and now, when I am a cripple, and not able to move, I am happier than I was in all my life before, or ever expect to be.[2]

Payson knew that God is the treasure found hidden in a field in the kingdom parables of Jesus. The man who found the treasure valued it above all else in his life. It caused him such great joy that he sold all he had in order to buy the field which contained it (Matt. 13:44). When we also value God highly, we can say with Edward Payson and the saints who have gone before us, "God is enough."

The Scriptures encourage us to find satisfaction in our relationship with God.

Satisfy us in the morning with your unfailing love, that we may sing for joy and be glad all our days.

—Psalm 90:14

When I awake, I will be satisfied with seeing your likeness.

—Psalm 17:15

Why spend money on what is not bread, and your labor on what does not satisfy? Listen, listen to me, and eat what is good, and your soul will delight in the richest of fare.

—Isaiah 55:2

Being satisfied leads to rest. When we are satisfied with a project or a job, we feel it is well done and we are at peace. Emotionally we are fulfilled, and we rest from our efforts. When we are satisfied after a meal, our stomachs are filled and we refuse another bite of food. Physically we are filled, and we rest.

God desires for us to be deeply satisfied in our souls. This soul satisfaction brings contentment and rest to our hearts and minds. He calls us to look to Him for this deep level of satisfaction, and by doing so, to learn that He is enough.

How do we learn to be satisfied? We begin by developing a thankful heart. But even more, we learn to be satisfied when we look beyond the circumstances of our lives to the One who controls them. When we look to God Himself and value Him as our greatest treasure, we find we need little else and we know the deepest satisfaction of all.

Be Still Before God

> Believing him to be a God all-sufficient, in him we must be entirely satisfied; let him be mine, and I have enough.[3]
>
> —Matthew Henry

Continue in your spiritual journal with these verses:

- Psalm 17:15
- Psalm 105:40
- Psalm 63:5
- Psalm 145:16
- Psalm 90:14
- Isaiah 53:11

10

Resting in God's Grace

⁓

A Christian is never in a state of completion but
always in the process of becoming.

—Martin Luther

*Being confident of this, that he who began a
good work in you will carry it on to completion
until the day of Christ Jesus.*

—Philippians 1:6

O ne of the added blessings of missionary life is being asked to share with others what God is doing in
the country where we work and in our lives. The problem is that even when we share quite honestly our difficulties, which include the lessons that God has taught
us, we come across sometimes as more spiritual than
we really are. Our messages hopefully inspire, but they
may also discourage.

On one of these occasions, I had just finished speaking to a group of women and was leaving the building

to go to my car. One of the older women from the group accompanied me to the parking lot. Petite and smartly dressed, she walked gracefully beside me, chatting about the meeting and not giving a hint about what was really on her mind. Before I opened the car door, however, she put her hand on my arm and said wistfully, "I try to be what I should be as a Christian, but I can't seem to do it. My faith isn't strong enough."

Her words are the echo of many a sincere Christian. What word is there for the one who, after the message is heard or the book is read, still "can't seem to do it?" For the one who, despite right desires and good intentions, continues to struggle to find time with the Lord or to have faith? Is the only course left to this dear woman to resign herself to a wistful glance at other seemingly stronger Christians or, worse yet, to gradually distance herself from God because of feelings of guilt or unworthiness?

No, the answer is not to be found in wistful longing nor in giving up altogether. The final word again is *rest*. Here, then, is a paradox of the Christian faith: that we strive to be all God has called us to be, but we do so while resting in His moment by moment grace towards us.

We certainly need His grace, because He has called us to nothing less than perfection. In the Sermon on the Mount, Jesus summed up a portion of His teaching with the words, "Be perfect, therefore, as your heavenly Father is perfect" (Matt. 5:48). I can imagine the lifted eyebrows and uneasy glances after He had uttered these words. Perfection is a tall order, even for the most sincere follower of Christ. But it is the standard given to us by the Lord Himself. We cannot ignore it.

Let me return to the woman who stood beside me in the parking lot. She knew God had a high standard of how we should live as Christians and she was feeling the weight of her inability to attain it, especially in the area of having faith.

I silently asked the Lord for wisdom, turned to her and said, "I know exactly what you mean. None of us can be what God wants us to be on our own, but do you know what I find very freeing? God knows it, too."

She looked confused, as well she might, so I continued, "Thank goodness we can be honest with God. He knows everything about us already, and that includes all the mistakes we make in trying to follow Him, the times we find it hard to trust, the things we find hard to obey. And because He already knows our imperfections, we can be honest with Him about our struggles. Tell Him about them, ask for His help, and then keep going."

I could have continued for some time, for the topic needed more than a few minutes spent in a parking lot, but the woman certainly left with something to think about concerning her view of herself before God. Focusing on her weak faith, she had become discouraged. By dwelling too much on her own failures, she had forgotten or perhaps not understood the truth of God's grace.

I think of my friend, Lisa, who has a right view of herself before God. She loves the Lord deeply and seeks to be all He has called her to be. Like the woman at the meeting, Lisa is fully aware of her weaknesses, but the difference is, she doesn't let them discourage her. I can still see her eyes shining when she commented during a Bible study on John 15, "Well, Jesus Himself said that apart from Him I can't do anything, so there!" It is very refreshing to be around someone like Lisa who is not trying to do everything and be everything but instead is resting in Christ.

Lisa accepts who she is, weaknesses and struggles included, and she is very honest about them. Her acceptance of her imperfections, however, doesn't keep her from pursuing holiness and obedience. It does enable her to rest in who she is before God. She knows, as I stated in a previous chapter, that she has nothing to hide (God knows it all anyway), nothing to prove (before God and others), and nothing to fear (from God and others). We, like Lisa, would do well to rest in who we are while moving towards becoming all we should be.

The question may well be asked, then, "Who are we?" We don't have to look far in Scripture to find the first part of the answer: We are sinners saved by grace.

The Scriptures are clear on this point (Rom. 3:10–12, 23–24; Eph. 2:1–9). We are not good people made better by our relationship with God. We are hopelessly bad people made good only by the mercy of God through Christ on the cross. It is freeing to admit this before God and each other. When we accept this truth about ourselves, we can rest, because we no longer have to prove otherwise, not to ourselves, not to others, and certainly not to God, who knew it all along. The burden of pretense is lifted and we are free to be ourselves; sinners, nothing more, saved by a gracious

God, in the company of other sinners who owe their very lives to the obedience of Christ in dying on the cross.

Admitting weakness and imperfection is neither an open door to a poor self-image nor an invitation to spiritual laziness. The apostle Paul was one of the most effective men for the Lord in his time. His walk with God was intimate and joyful, and if anyone was single-minded for Christ, it was Paul. But he also referred to himself as the worst of sinners (1 Tim. 1:15–16). Did he suffer from low self-esteem? I doubt it, when he could also write the bold assertion, "I can do everything through him who gives me strength" (Phil. 4:13). Did he decide that since he was obviously so weak, he may as well not try? Certainly not, for he is the same man who wrote, "Forgetting what is behind and straining toward what is ahead, I press on toward the goal to win the prize for which God has called me heaven-ward in Christ Jesus" (Phil. 3:13–14).

Paul also wrote, "being confident of this, that he who began a good work in you will carry it on to comple-tion until the day of Christ Jesus" (Phil. 1:6).

The work of Christ in us begins at the point of the cross when we accept that we are sinners saved only by God's grace. At the cross we change our status from sinner to saint and from there we begin the journey of faith. The second truth about ourselves is for the jour-ney itself: We are a people in process.

We are saints, true, but on this side of heaven, imper-fect ones at best. We are not yet what we should be, but we are on our way, and God has never expected us to make the journey on our own strength and abilities. God

Himself, who began the work in us, is the One who will carry it on to completion. Paul writes to encourage the church at Philippi, "For it is God who works in you to will and to act according to his good purpose" (Phil. 2:13). God Himself is at work in us both to will, that is to have the intention, and to act, to have the ability, to do His will. There is hope, then, for our imperfections. We can rest in who we are as imperfect people because we are in the process of being made perfect by the One who saved us, called us, and set us on the journey. So when we struggle, we call on His strength to help us through. When we doubt, we go freely to Him, being honest about all doubts, questions, and fears, because He knows them anyway. When we fail to trust, we ask Him to give us the faith that we lack. When we stumble and fall on the journey, we rely on His grace and the work accomplished at the cross to set us on our feet again.

Brother Lawrence had a wonderfully light heart before God, probably because he believed fully in the grace of God. When he sinned, he went immediately to the Lord and asked for pardon, then he went on with his work without troubling himself any more. "We ought not to be discouraged on account of our sins," he advised, "rather, simply pray for the Lord's grace with perfect confidence, relying upon the infinite mercies of the Lord Jesus Christ. God has never failed offering us His grace at each action."

This is not to suggest that Brother Lawrence thought lightly of sin, and neither should we. One needs only to read through the Old Testament prophets to realize how serious God is about sin in the lives of His people. In the New Testament, Jesus told a parable to illustrate the right attitude in prayer before God. In the parable of two men praying at the temple, one man saw only his righteousness and felt superior to others who sinned, while the other man felt the weight of his sin so deeply that he couldn't even look up to heaven. He could only plead, "God, have mercy on me, a sinner" (Luke 18:9–14). Only the second man, who admitted his sinful state and grieved because of it, received grace from God.

Brother Lawrence's peace before God came not because he thought lightly of sin, but because he thought highly of God. He took God at His Word when he read, "If we confess our sins, he is faithful and just and will forgive us our sins and purify us from all unrighteousness" (1 John 1:9). Acting on God's promise, he sought God's grace and never doubted that he received it.

We have the same grace available to us each moment of each day, not as an excuse to sin, but as a means of keeping sin from hindering our going forward with Christ. When we keep short accounts of our sin and failures in the Christian life by bringing them honestly and immediately to the cross, then we maintain our intimacy with Christ and we continue, unburdened, on the journey.

Resting in who we are, in light of these observations, brings us back to a core truth of this book. We can rest in who we are, ultimately, because we rest in who God is. He knows us thoroughly and, despite what He knows, loves us and freely extends to us His grace, not once at the cross but as often as we come to Him with a sincere desire for forgiveness.

"My grace is sufficient for you" were His words to

Paul when the apostle struggled with an affliction painful enough for him to call a "thorn in the flesh." "My grace is sufficient to you" is God's promise to us in the face of our own "thorns," spiritual or physical. They are liberating words because they enable us to rest from striving by our own abilities to be worthy of His calling. We simply know that we can't. But the truth of our inability is not discouraging, because we know that He is able. "My grace is sufficient for you" is encouraging because it brings hope for the journey. Yes, we are imperfect now, but we do not need to remain in our imperfections. God is doing something about them. We are not yet what we should be, but we are on our way. He will indeed carry on His work until completion, and when the journey is over, we will stand before the Lord saved by His grace and made perfect by His own hand.

Will you accept God's invitation to rest in the quiet center?

Be Still Before God

> We ought, without any anxiety, to expect the pardon of our sins from the blood of the Lord Jesus Christ: our only endeavor should be to love Him with all our hearts.
>
> —Brother Lawrence

Write in your journal the areas in which you have difficulty following Christ fully. Ask God to give you what you need in order to be obedient in these areas. Ask Him to reveal to you any sinful actions or attitudes which need to be confessed. Receive His forgiveness and continue the day in awareness of His grace.

Verses for meditation:

- John 1:16–17
- Hebrews 2:18
- Romans 5:8
- Hebrews 7:25
- 1 Corinthians 1:8–9
- 2 Timothy 1:12
- Jude 24–25

Endnotes

Chapter One

1. Thomas R. Kelly, *A Testament of Devotion* (New York: HarperCollins, 1992), 3.
2. Corrie ten Boom, *Clippings from My Notebook* (Nashville: Thomas Nelson, 1982), 108.
3. Reprinted from *Knowing God* by J. I. Packer, page 37. Copyright 1973 by J. I. Packer. Used by permission of InterVarsity Press, P.O. Box 1400, Downers Grove, IL 60515.
4. Ibid., 26.
5. Taken from *Prayer: Conversing with God* by Rosalind Rinker (Grand Rapids: Zondervan, 1959), 23.

Chapter Two

1. Taken from *The God of All Comfort* by Hannah Whitall Smith (Moody Bible Institute of Chicago, Moody Press, 1956), 107.
2. Ibid.
3. Ibid., 116.
4. Ibid., 121.

Chapter Three

1. Henri J. M. Nouwen, *The Way of the Heart: Desert Spirituality and Contemporary Ministry* (New York: HarperCollins, 1981), 31.
2. Kelly, *A Testament of Devotion*, 97.

Chapter Four

1. Nouwen, *The Way of the Heart: Desert Spirituality and Contemporary Ministry*, 30.
2. Matthew Henry, *The Secret of Communion with God* (Grand Rapids: Kregel, 1991), 24.
3. Ibid.
4. Ibid., 25.
5. Ibid.

Chapter Five

1. Taken from Andrew Murray, *The Inner Chamber* (Ft. Washington, Pa.: Christian Literature Crusade, 1981), 19.
2. Quotes from Brother Lawrence and Frank Laubach in this chapter are taken from Frank Laubach, *Practicing His Presence* (Golete, Calif.: Christian Books, 1973), 23.
3. *The Practice of the Presence of God,* by Brother Lawrence, continues to be one of the most influential spiritual classics of all time. See the version edited and paraphrased by Donald E. Demaray (Grand Rapids: Baker, 1975).
4. Laubach, *Practicing His Presence*, 23.
5. Ibid.
6. Kelly, *A Testament of Devotion*, 98, 33–34.
7. Taken from David McCasland, *Oswald Chambers:*

Abandoned to God (Nashville, Tenn.: Discovery House, 1993), 287.

Chapter Six

1. A. W. Tozer, *The Pursuit of God* (Alberta, Canada: Horizon House, 1976), 91.
2. Taken from Elisabeth Elliot, *Keep a Quiet Heart*, (Ann Arbor, Mich.: Servant, 1995), 98. Used by permission.
3. Ibid., 99.
4. Kelly, *A Testament of Devotion*, 45.
5. Taken from Hannah Whitall Smith, *The Christian's Secret of a Happy Life* (Old Tappan, N.J.: Spire Books/Revell, 1942), 101–3.
6. Elliot, *Keep a Quiet Heart*, 140.

Chapter Seven

1. Elliot, *Keep a Quiet Heart*, 135.
2. Elisabeth Elliot, *All That Ever Was Ours* (Grand Rapids: Revell, 1987), 27.
3. Amy Carmichael, *Candles in the Dark* (Ft. Washington, Pa.: Christian Literature Crusade, 1981).
4. Faith Cook, *Singing in the Fire* (Carlisle, Pa.: The Banner of Truth Trust, 1995), 8.
5. Ibid., 44.
6. Taken from Corrie ten Boom, *Clippings from My Notebook* (Nashville: Thomas Nelson, 1982).
7. Keven D. Miller, "Gritty Pioneers," *Christian History*, no. 52, 36.
8. Taken from *How I Know God Answers Prayer* by Rosalind Goforth, page 80. © Ontario Bible College and Theological Seminary, (Elkhart, Ind.: Bethel, n.d.).

9. Ibid., 122.
10. Amy Carmichael, *If; His Thoughts Said . . . His Father Said* (London: Triangle/SPCK, 1987), 16.
11. Ibid.

Chapter Eight
1. Hannah Whitall Smith.

Chapter Nine
1. Taken from Thomas à Kempis, *The Imitation of Christ* (Chicago: Moody, 1980), 114.
2. Cook, *Singing in the Fire.*
3. Henry, *The Secret of Communion with God,* 48.

The Spiritual Woman

10 Steps to Spirituality in a Demanding World

by Lewis and Betty Drummond
Foreword by Ruth Bell Graham

This collection of biographies and devotional reflections illustrates ten steps that women can take to attain deeper spirituality and greater closeness to God. The stories of these women's struggles and victories will challenge and encourage the reader on her quest to be a Spirit-led woman of God.

0-8254-2469-0

Kay Arthur	"Growing in God"
Vonetta Bright	"Sharing God"
Jill Briscoe	"Knowing God"
Evelyn Christenson	"Talking with God"
Elisabeth Elliot Gren	"Loving God"
Martha Franks	"Exemplifying God"
Anne Graham Lotz	"Overflowing with God"
Henrietta Mears	"Serving God"
Jessie Penn-Lewis	"Abiding in God"
Amanda Smith	"Submitting to God"

Women of Awakenings

The Historic Contribution of Women to Revival Movements

by Lewis and Betty Drummond
Foreword by Anne Graham Lotz

Lewis and Betty Drummond begin with Deborah in the book of Judges and trace the historic role of women in revivals through the great awakenings of the last three centuries. Included are chapters on Susanna Wesley, Catherine Booth, Amy Carmichael, Bertha Smith, and Ruth Bell Graham.

"These are ordinary women like you and me who simply walked in faith. . . . It is my prayer that God will use this book to revive you."
—Kay Arthur

0-8254-2474-7

"Books that model women of faith make a difference in an upside down culture. . . . This book helps."

—Jill Briscoe

"This book gives us not only the biblical and historical evidence of God using women in past revivals, but the possibility of God doing it again. What a timely and encouraging book!"

—Evelyn Christenson

A Woman's Guide to Keeping Promises

Fifty-Two Ways to Choose Happiness and Fulfillment

by Judith Rolfs

While men's movements have emphasized the responsibilities of Christian men in society and the home, Judith Rolfs is deeply concerned that Christian women find equally creative ways to deepen their spiritual lives and honor their responsibilities to God, themselves, and others. Some of the fifty-two chapters include:

0-8254-3627-3

Deepening Friendships
Respecting Your Mate
Preventing Family Problems
Keeping the Joy
Releasing Creativity
Surviving Your Husband's Life Crises
Leading Others to Christ
Aging with Grace
Equipping Children
Hearing God
Being a Grandma

Her experience as a Christian counselor, wife, and mother provides an insightful perspective on the challenges and opportunities of today's single women, wives, and mothers

Women Who Changed the Heart of the City

The Untold Story of the City Rescue Mission Movement

by Delores T. Burger

For forty years, there have been more than five hundred city rescue missions in the United States and Canada. Prominent in this movement have been courageous, yet seldom recognized, women who tackled the worst social problems of the day while maintaining a household and raising children. Learn about their inspiring stories.

0-8254-2146-2

"This book, written by my friend and a choice servant of Christ, should encourage, inspire, and provide a powerful apologetic to secular society on the importance of the Christian faith lived out by caring people."
—Charles W. Colson

"In an age where women are looking to make a difference, *Women Who Changed the Heart of the City* is right on target!"
—Florence Littauer

"Everyone loves a story . . . and this is what Delores Burger provides us with in her book."
—Kay Arthur